AIRMAIL
how it all began

Other Books by the Author

The Doolittle Raid
Round-the-World Flights
From the Wright Brothers to the Astronauts
The Modern U.S. Air Force
The Compact History of the U.S. Air Force
Doolittle's Tokyo Raiders
Four Came Home
Air Rescue! (with W.F. Moseley)
Helicopter Rescues
The Complete Guide for the Serviceman's Wife
Grand Old Lady (with W.F. Moseley)
Our Family Affairs
The DC-3: The Story of a Fabulous Airplane
Lighter-Than-Air Flight
Polar Aviation
Minutemen of the Air
The Legendary DC-3
The Wright Brothers: Pioneers of Power Flight
The First Book of the Moon
Jimmy Doolittle: Master of the Calculated Risk
The Saga of the Air Mail
Attack on Yamamoto

AIRMAIL

how it all began
Carroll V. Glines

TAB **AERO**

Blue Ridge Summit, PA

TO THE AIRMAIL PIONEERS . . .

who blazed the nation's aerial trails
and proved that man and his mail
could be flown from place to place
on schedule, swiftly, reliably, and safely.

FIRST EDITION
FIRST PRINTING

Copyright © 1990 by TAB BOOKS
Printed in the United States of America

Library of Congress Cataloging-in-Publication Data

Glines, Carroll V., 1920 –
    Airmail—how it all began / by Carroll V. Glines
      p.   cm.
    ISBN 0-8306-3378-2 (pbk.)
    1. Air mail service—United States—History. I. Title.
    HE6496.G49   1990
    383'.144'0973—dc20   89-18187
                                         CIP

Acquisitions Editor: Jeff Worsinger
Book Editor: Norval G. Kennedy
Production: Katherine Brown

Contents

Foreword vi

Acknowledgments viii

Introduction ix

1 The Pigeon Post 1

2 Lighter-Than-Air Mail 17

3 The U.S. Airmail Begins 33

4 The Glory Years 57

5 Tales of the Airmail Service 71

6 The Airlines Are Born 95

7 Critical Months:
   The Army Takes Over 107

8 Airmail Firsts 123

9 Airmail Philately 141

10 Missile Mail 147

   Index 157

Foreword

Each day of the year, thousands of passengers board airliners all over the world and fly in luxurious comfort to their destinations. In each plane, bags of mail are stowed just before take-off, off-loaded after landing and rushed to the local post office almost before the passengers can collect their baggage. Passengers and crew rarely give a thought to the mail that is on board. Yet, neither the airplane nor the airline would be operating were it not for the original development of airmail routes by the United States Post Office Department.

Few people realize what the pilots who flew the mail for the Post Office Department between May 15, 1918 and August 31, 1927, contributed to aviation progress. The airlines of today owe their very existence to the skill and persistence of these pilots in carrying the mail through the skies when many defeatists said it couldn't be done. Much of the aviation equipment we take for granted today, such as aircraft radios, air navigation aids, instruments and landing lights, as well as many of the safety devices used in modern aircraft, were pioneered and improved by these intrepid flyers. It was these pilots who proved that regular schedules could be flown regardless of the weather, day or night, over any terrain and with reasonable safety. In fact, they proved the point so well that people wanted to ride with the mail, even at great personal discomfort. And, to the surprise of the pilots and the mail line owners, people were also willing to pay for the privilege. So it was that the airline industry was born.

The price of aviation progress has never been cheap. Many of the early pilots died trying to meet their schedules. They died because either their proficiency or their planes were no match for the weather they encountered or they suffered the bad luck of faulty engines or airframes. But with each crash and each death, a lesson was learned by other pilots, who demanded better equipment of the manufacturers and better proficiency of themselves. The result was a continually better safety record, more reliable schedules, faster planes and, to the delight of many entrepreneurs, profits.

This book is a fitting tribute, not only to the band of men who started it all officially in 1918, but also to the balloon and dirigible pilots as well who tried to be first in the lighter-than-air days. To them all we owe more than we realize.

Robert C. Reeve
Chairman of the Board, President and Founder
Reeve Aleutian Airways, Inc.
Anchorage, Alaska

Acknowledgments

The material for this book came from many sources—the Library of Congress, National Air and Space Museum, Air Force Archives, and organizations such as the Air Transport Association, the airlines and aircraft manufacturers. The richest source of all was an organization known as the Air Mail Pioneers made up of the survivors of those glory years when the Air Service and the Post Office Department flew the mail. Men like Luther Harris, Ernest M. Allison, Dean C. Smith, Emil Henrich, J.W. Hackbarth and other members of the Western Division were especially cooperative in providing stories and material.

Special mention and the author's particular thanks are due Robert C. "Bob" Reeve, famous Alaskan bush pilot and late president of Reeve Aleutian Airways. Bob's continuing encouragement and assistance paved the way for me to locate airmail stories and meet many of the original Air Mail Pioneers to whom the aviation industry owes so much.

I am also indebted to Major Reuben H. Fleet for an account of the days in 1918 when the Air Service began the airmail experiment. And to Major General Benjamin D. Foulois, former chief of the Air Corps, for his recounting of the days when the Army flew the mail in 1934.

Acknowledgment is also made to Robert I. Stanfield, editor and publisher of *Popular Aviation,* for permission to use the article by John Goldstrom entitled "The Uncovered Wagon" from an early issue. My thanks also go to Robert B. Pitkin for permission to use material I prepared for *American Legion Magazine* under the title of "The Golden Anniversary of the Air Mail."

Carroll V. Glines
McLean, Virginia

Introduction

The story of the development of the airmail begins far before the invention of the airplane, the dirigible, or even the balloon. It begins with the pigeon post, which was used by armies many years before the birth of Christ to send messages long distances. Since then, men have used all the vehicles of the air to carry letters from one place to another. Lighter-than-air craft—the balloon and dirigible—carried mail. Then came the airplane. Now, in the Space Age, experiments are being conducted with missile mail. Soon, we can expect interplanetary rocket mail as men explore the frontiers of space.

The story of the airmail as we know it today began on May 15, 1918, when the first official airmail route in the world was opened between New York and Washington, D.C., with a stop at Philadelphia. The distance of the route was 218 miles, and one round trip per day was made, six days a week. Air Service pilots flew the route until August 12, 1918, when the Post Office Department took over the entire operation, furnishing its own planes and pilots.

Flights on regular schedule, in all kinds of weather, presented new problems, but gradually difficulties were overcome and an encouraging percentage of successful flights was attained. Once proven, service expanded until it covered most of the larger cities of the United States.

As the Post Office Department pilots proved the practicability of scheduled airmail service on a national scale, operations were transferred to private operators in 1926 and 1927. But even in 1927 the idea of air mail still had to be sold to a skeptical public. Most businessmen sent carbon copies of their letters by train "just in case." With their newly-won airmail contracts, the airlines went to work in earnest to fire up national interest in sending letters by air.

It was inevitable that people would attempt to get themselves transported as efficiently as their mail. They came singly at first, usually on life-or-death trips which demanded speed. The airmail operators treated the first passengers as interlopers and nuisances but soon began to realize that a passenger fare was "gravy" income since they had to make the flights anyhow in accordance with their mail contracts.

Developments were rapid after 1927. Two-passenger planes were replaced with larger craft capable of carrying 12 passengers. The idea of regular passenger service which could be as reliable as the mail service had proven to be was not only possible, but was fully accepted by the traveling public.

The years 1927 and 1928 marked the greatest boom era in commercial aviation up to that time. Colonel Charles A. Lindbergh's tour of the country urging chambers of commerce, city councils, and civic organizations to establish airports and pointing out to them the rapid growth and the advantages and value of commercial air transportation to each community, had a far-reaching effect on the growth of contract airmail service. Airports soon sprang up all over the country, and the Post Office Department was flooded with petitions and delegations requesting airmail service through their communities.

In 1938 Congress passed the McCarran-Lee Bill, better known as the Civil Aeronautics Act, which regulated the burgeoning air transport industry and made it a full-fledged partner in the nation's transportation system. The Act required the airlines to serve the nation by contributing to the postal service, interstate commerce, and national defense. Slowly but surely the airmail became a profitable operation for the Government. Today, airmail service has become so efficient that we expect a letter to fly half-way around the world in a single day, and we tend to forget that it was only three-quarters of a century ago that this service officially was begun.

Postmaster General William T. Barry remarked in 1834 that "the celerity of the mail should always be equal to the most rapid transition of the traveler." Little did he realize that the transition of the traveler would one day reach supersonic speeds.

In the pages that follow, the story of the airmail will be told in detail. It is a story of courage, persistence, and ingenuity. It is told as a tribute to the airmail pioneers who gave the world a new industry and proved that flying could be made safe, dependable, and profitable.

= 1 =

THE PIGEON POST

THE REAL PIONEERS of the airmail were not men but pigeons. The Bible tells us that a dove brought Noah an olive leaf as evidence that the flood had subsided and that he soon would be safe with his ark-load of animals. This dove was no doubt the progenitor of the homing pigeons we know today.

The use of pigeons for carrying messages was prevalent as long as 3,000 years ago. Clay tablets with Babylonian hieroglyphics were found in Egypt proving that a pigeon postal service was in use 1,400 years before Christ. And it is known that King Solomon sent mail by pigeon messenger in 1000 B.C.

The ancient Greeks used a pigeon courier device to relay the results of the Olympic Games in Athens to the outlying cities. The contestants and their fans would take their own pigeons to the Games and release them after the events in which they had participated. Their townsmen, knowing when the pigeons were to be released in Athens, would wait breathlessly around the home lofts for the news. This service was well developed by the Greeks during the Golden Age of Greece and was probably the source of the idea for the Romans. The famous Greek poet Anacreon wrote his "Ode to the Carrier Pigeon" in 560 B.C. which documented the role of these feathered mailmen for posterity.

Julius Caesar used homing pigeons extensively during his Gallic campaign. Each day he would release a postal pigeon with a letter tied around its neck. The aerial courier would arrive at its home loft where copies would be made of the message and delivered by relay pigeons to several other destinations simultaneously. Thus, Caesar's countrymen knew of his successes literally within hours of the battles and on a regular and frequent basis.

While the early recorded history of the pigeon post is at best fragmentary, it is well established that the first commercial pigeon post as a mail service was begun by the Sultan Nurreddin, Caliph of Baghdad, in A.D. 1146. He appointed "postmasters" in the larger cities and towns and maintained a regular service all over his country as well as with Egypt and Syria. Towers were built along the routes for watchmen, who were to look out for the pigeons and care for them. An even more efficient service was maintained by the Caliph Achmed at the end of the 12th century.

The pigeon post was used in Europe in 1573 at the siege of Haarlem when William of Orange sent a homing pigeon toward the city. It fell into the hands of the Spaniards, who realized for the first time how valuable these couriers were. After that, the Spaniards posted lookouts who tried to kill every bird, regardless of species, that flew over their lines. The next year a pigeon was credited with saving the Dutch forces at Leyden by carrying a message for help when the defenders of the city were at the point of surrender to the Spanish.

In peacetime, homing pigeons were used in Europe to carry information concerning the results of horse races, lotteries, and cock fights to bettors in outlying areas. Businessmen, always anxious to compress the time factor in the conduct of their affairs, used the pigeon post extensively. During the years of the successes of Napoleon, Nathan Rothschild of London established pigeon posts in France, Belgium, and Holland. He equipped his agents with cages of pigeons and sent them to the continent to follow Napoleon's armies. The men would report the results of Napoleon's campaigns back to Rothschild by these winged messengers so that the great speculator could invest in some new venture or divest himself of a losing proposition before his competitors were aware of what had happened. His foreknowledge enabled him to increase his fortune to the constant chagrin of his business rivals.

Rothchild's successful courier service, once known, was easily copied. Leading banking houses in London, Paris, and Brussels employed pigeon raisers to establish service between the three capitals to keep them informed of the fluctuations in the stock and money exchanges. These pigeons were called *Kurstauben* (exchange pigeons) and were a vital link in the com-

Gallant John Silver, famous World War I homing pigeon, lost a leg while carrying a vital message from the front lines in France. He is on permanent display at the Air Force Museum, Wright-Patterson AFB, Ohio.

munication system of the day. During the French Revolution in 1848, accounts of what happened in Paris were carried by pigeons and the messages they bore were published almost as quickly in English and Belgian papers as in the Paris journals.

The advent of the telegraph threatened to make the pigeon post obsolete. Baron Paul Reuter established a telegraph line between Berlin and Aix-la-Chapelle. However, for technical reasons, he could not complete the link from Aix-la-Chapelle to Brussels. To fill this gap, Reuter used a pigeon post which saved over eight hours in transmission time. This pigeon post did much to establish the fame of Reuter's telegraphic news service, which is still in being today.

Another of man's inventions figured in the history of the use of pigeons as messengers. France, pushed into war with Prussia in 1870, found itself overwhelmed by Prussian forces. In order to get information out of the surrounded city of Paris, two old balloons previously used at fairs and circuses were pressed into service. One of them, piloted by aeronaut Jules Duruof, was able to be lofted into the air at night and the word of the plight of Paris was spread. The success of this balloon, the *Neptune*, encouraged the Parisians to construct more.

At the same time, pigeon fanciers suggested to the military authorities that the pigeons within the city limits be sent out by these balloons and that others from the provinces be sent into the city by the same means.

The manufacture of the balloons in the city enabled the first part of the plan to be put into action quickly. Over 350 pigeons were airlifted out of Paris in the next few weeks. Of these only 57 returned. These few, however, bore letters on the newly-invented microfilm. The new process was so successful that 200 letters could be reduced to a piece of film that weighed only one-eighth of a grain. Copies of complete newspapers were carried by these few birds.

While a few balloons could get out and a few pigeons could get into Paris, a reverse service was also attempted. A pigeon post service was established at Tours for the purpose of conveying messages into the capital city. The birds, carrying microfilm, could carry about $500 worth of dispatches for businessmen and others willing to pay the price. During the latter days of the four-month siege, the Prussians introduced trained hawks that were sent aloft to attack and kill the pigeons. But just as every weapon of war has had its counter-weapon, the plucky French attached bamboo whistles to the tails of their messengers. This device, invented by the Chinese, made a weird noise when the pigeon was airborne and frightened the hawks away.*

Eventually, the French rallied a large army, and in May, 1871, the Prussians negotiated a cease-fire and withdrew to their borders. The famous City of Light, which would be besieged in other wars in other times, was saved by a vehicle of the air and the feathered mailmen who had done so much to sustain the hope and faith of a nation. It has been estimated that the successful combination of balloon and homing pigeons enabled 115,000 official military messages and over one million letters between private citizens to be exchanged.

German lighthouse keepers used pigeons in 1876 to announce the arrival of ships and summon aid in times of emergency. In 1897, a commercial pigeon post was established by the Great Barrier Pigeongram Service between the Great Barrier Islands and Auckland, New Zealand, a distance of 65 miles. This service was successfully and uninterruptedly operated until 1908 when an underwater cable was laid. Other pigeon posts have been used at one time or another in the United States, Australia, India, and Poland.

While peacetime use of homing pigeons was limited because of the improvement of the telegraph and the invention of the radio telephone, the military services of the world continued to utilize them. In the South African War from 1899 to 1902, British forces employed pigeons to carry messages during the sieges of Kimberly, Mafeking, and Ladysmith. In 1904, the Japanese, then engaged in the Russo-Japanese War, discovered that

---

*This same device was used as late as World War II by American forces.

homers could be hauled for many miles in mobile lofts and would return to their new homes with very little training. This discovery had come about because a Japanese officer had observed that pigeons kept aboard ship by fishermen would always return to their vessels after being released elsewhere, even though the vessels had been moved 10 to 20 miles in the interim.

The United States Army considered the use of homing pigeons for messengers following the Civil War. Brigadier General Nelson A. Miles, commanding cavalry units operating in the northwestern areas, was given a dozen birds to experiment with in 1879. They bred rapidly and "when I left Fort Keough, numbered about fifty." His experiments were successful although at times "we were troubled by a small hawk, which greatly disturbed the birds in their flight, occasionally destroying them." He noted that the longest distance made was about one hundred miles, from the mouth of the Big Horn River to Fort Keough, Montana.

Although other Army officers recommended that pigeons be trained to maintain communications between outposts, especially where the telegraph ran through hostile Indian country, there is little evidence that they were because of the shortage of funds and the difficulties of transporting and training them to serve a useful military purpose. But European armies did not abandon the pigeon post even though the telegraph had been improved, the airplane had been invented and used successfully as an observation vehicle, and radio had proved its potential for military use. When World War I began, all of the armies engaged had large numbers of trained birds in efficiently organized units. Their value was proven many times in battle.

A French officer, required to write a report on the work of pigeons after the Battle of Verdun, noted:

> Experience has proved that telephone and radio liaison is often interrupted in the zone of advance; information sent by runners is always delayed on account of the state of the terrain and the violence of barrage fire; visual signals are sometimes obscured by smoke and dust and are then inefficacious; aerial observation is often subject to unfavorable conditions on account of bad weather or the distance of the objectives, and is not able to give the command accurate information concerning the progress of the battle.
>
> Pigeons can work regularly and, in spite of bombardments, dust, smoke, or fog, bring accurate details concern-

ing the situation of the troops in action within a relatively short span of time.

Liaison by pigeons has rendered inestimable service ever since the beginning of the battle of Verdun. It has won the appreciation of the high command and line officers, and its general adoption is advisable.

The first extensive use of homing pigeons by American troops in World War I was during the Aisne-Marne offensive in 1918. Due to the rapid advance of American troops and the constantly changing front line, difficulty was experienced in settling the birds, but a mobile loft operating near the line received 78 important messages and 148 test messages in the active period extending from August 29th to September 11th. Of the 72 birds used at this loft, not a single one failed to return.

In the St. Mihiel drive which followed, 567 American birds were used in battle. Many of these were assigned to tank units and, although their training had been brief, and fog and rain made flying difficult, 90 important messages were received. Twenty-four of the birds were lost or killed in action.

On September 21, 1918, training of birds for use in the Meuse-Argonne offensive was begun. Because of the hurried notice of pending attack, only five days were available to condition the birds for their work. Over 400 American birds were used during this offensive and 403 vital messages were delivered by the pigeons. The distances flown varied from 20 to 50 kilometers. In spite of the difficulties, caused by the constantly changing battlefront, less than ten percent of the faithful birds failed to complete their missions.

There were many heroes among pigeons who faithfully served their countries during the First World War, and their exploits have become legendary. One of these was a pigeon who was nameless until he lost his leg in battle; from then on he became known as John Silver.

The story of John Silver began in January, 1918, when Army records show that he was hatched in an American Signal Corps pigeon loft behind the lines in France. He spent his first weeks learning the gentle art of flying and homing. He learned to carry a small metal cannister strapped to his leg and fly unerringly back to his loft in spite of the noise of gunfire and bad weather. Upon "graduation" he was assigned to a front-line infantry unit for courier duty. His first messages were relatively unimportant so that if he became confused and fell into enemy hands, no vital information would be lost. When his company

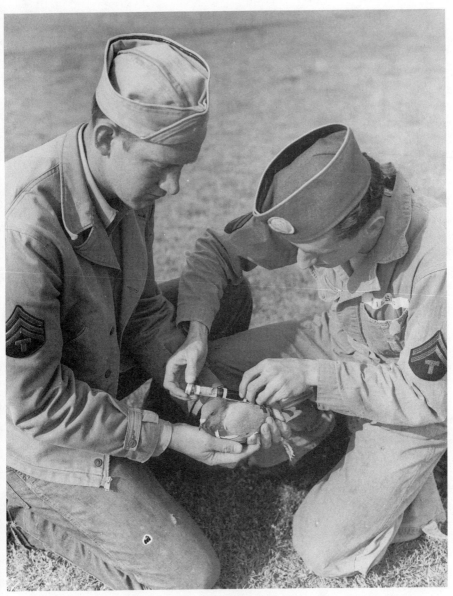

The large capsule attached to the pigeon's back was used to carry messages, photos, and maps during World War II in Europe.

Small capsules were attached to a pigeon's leg containing messages written on tissue paper.

commander was satisfied that John was reliable, he was given more important messages to carry.

From the first, John's exceptional skill at dodging artillery barrages was noted. Time after time, when the shelling was especially heavy and a message had to be sent rearward, John got through. On several occasions, he was the only one of several pigeon couriers that survived the mission.

It was on October 21, 1918, at exactly 2:35 P.M. that John Silver was released from a front-line trench near Grand Pre. The now-famous Meuse-Argonne drive had begun and the rear headquarters at Rampont, 40 kilometers away, had to be notified of the rapidly changing battle situation to prevent accidental artillery shelling of American positions. The Germans were laying down an intense barrage of their own before a massive attack, and John's unit needed help.

When the tiny aluminum cannister was fastened on his leg and John was released, the tense, battle-tired soldiers watched anxiously because their lives depended on his getting through. John fluttered briefly along the ground after his release, started

Paratroopers often took pigeons with them as they parachuted into combat zones. Pvt. Arthur W. Goodrich of the Parachute Training Regiment displays pigeons in a corselet.

toward the German lines for a few yards, then turned toward the rear as he climbed and leveled off at tree-top height. The men below shouted their encouragement, but suddenly gasped when they saw a shell explode near him.

The blast threw the pitifully small gray and white body upward for a hundred feet amid a shower of mud and feathers. John plunged earthward momentarily, then flapped his wings wildly to regain his balance and continued on his way. The men watching felt sure that John had been badly hurt and would never make it back to headquarters.

Twenty-five minutes after he was released, John flopped onto his loft landing at Rampont, more dead than alive. Miraculously, he had covered the distance at a speed of 60 miles per hour. A machine-gun bullet had pierced his breast, bits of shrapnel had ripped mercilessly into the tiny body, and his right leg was missing. The message tube, however, was dangling from the ligaments of his torn left leg. He had successfully completed his mission in spite of his wounds and the besieged unit was saved.

The men of John's Signal Company nursed the gallant messenger back to health. The stump of his leg healed and he could still fly. His gallantry was contagious, and the men refused to let him be retired or destroyed. Instead, he became an inspiration and acquired the name of "John Silver," after the one-legged pirate in Robert Louis Stevenson's *Treasure Island*.

John Silver was kept in the Signal Corps and was eventually transferred to Schofield Barracks, Hawaii, where he stayed until his death on December 6, 1935, at the age of 17 years, 11 months—a remarkably old age for a pigeon. Today, this brave airman can be seen at the Air Force Museum at Wright-Patterson Air Force Base, Ohio, where he stands tall and straight in the Hall of Fame.

There were many other pigeon heroes among the 20,000 used by American troops in World War I.* The Mocker distinguished himself along the Beaumont front when, with one eye destroyed by shrapnel and his head a welter of clotted blood, he carried a message of vital importance to the rear. His information provided American artillerymen with the data needed to pinpoint the location of several German batteries which were causing great losses on advancing American troops.

Another pigeon hero, named President Wilson, was launched from the front lines toward his loft at Cuisy on Novem-

---

*The other Allies used over 300,000 pigeons. The Germans and their co-belligerants had about 150,000 birds assigned to the armed forces.

ber 5, 1918, and flew through heavy fog to get his message to the rear. Peppered with shrapnel and also minus a leg, he delivered his message and saved more American lives.

In spite of the advances made in radio between wars, there was still a need for homing pigeons during World War II. Again, as in past wars, all the fighting nations used them to advantage, to supplement other forms of communication. The homers again proved their value in carrying messages when radios failed or couldn't be used. Aircraft crews carried them on long overwater missions, and they were used in airfield-to-airfield and island-to-island communications, especially over enemy-held territory. Pigeons were dropped by parachute to isolated units, thus enabling them to communicate without giving away their position.

Many experiments were carried out, and some interesting developments were forthcoming. To the surprise of pigeon fanciers some birds were trained to fly at night, and others were moved thousands of miles and taught to home on their new base after only a few weeks. Another major achievement was the training of "two-way" birds that could fly to a point 75 miles away *and return.*

The Army Air Forces of the United States brought the state of the pigeon flying art to its highest level during World War II. Pigeon units were organized into companies in February, 1943, and men, called "pigeoneers," were assigned to train the 20,000 birds procured for world-wide use. Major Thomas MacClure, an ex-prospector who used pigeons to stake his claim records from mine locations in the wilderness to registration offices in nearby towns, was appointed Chief of the Pigeon Service.

Pigeons for AAF use were carried in special containers which had room for two, four, or more birds. Each container also had a section for a message book, map overlays, message capsules, pencils, and bird food. The usual procedure, if there was time, was to release one pigeon while in flight, and another after a crash landing or ditching. It was thought that it would be a considerable shock to a 14-ounce bird to be tossed out into the slip stream of a four-engine airplane going over 200 miles an hour, but the birds weathered it. Usually, the pigeon was wrapped in a split paper sack and released, head facing forward. Pressure of the slip stream held the bird's wings close to his body until he dropped clear. Then the bird fought his way out of the bag, spiralled down to his favorite altitude of 300–400 feet, and set out for home.

Pigeoneers load a bird into a cannister attached to Sir, one of many war dogs used during World War II.

A homing pigeon with message is tossed out of a scout plane by an observer during war maneuvers in the 1930s. Since few open cockpit planes had radios during the days before World War II, pigeons were used to report activities of "enemy" ground units.

There were many instances of pigeon messengers being used by United States ground forces in the South Pacific, North Africa, Italy, and France. In Italy, for example, a homer named G.I. Joe saved a British unit at Colvi Vecchio from a bombing attack. At Foggia, huge B-17 Flying Fortresses were lining up for take-off on a mission to bomb the city located along the Volturno River.

Just as the lead plane was about to thunder down the runway, the mission was called off and the pilots ordered to return to the briefing room. The operations officer told the assembled pilots that the British had just taken Colvi Vecchio.

The officer had gotten the news from G.I. Joe, who had flown over blasted forests, smashed villages, and through the brain-numbing barrages of artillery. He was unharmed and dropped into his cote, where an alert sergeant took the life-saving capsule message from his leg.

The British Government also honored many heroic pigeons who delivered vital messages during wartime. A Roll of Honour

Chapter 1

Pigeon is released from open hatch of a Douglas B-18 bomber before a submarine patrol in the Caribbean.

was established in the Imperial War Museum in London, and the names of pigeons who served valiantly are listed. For those who displayed exceptional acts of heroism, a special medal was struck. Known as the Dickin Medal, it is the only decoration for furred and feathered heroes instituted during World War II and is only awarded on official recommendation.

Although the day of the pigeon mailman seems at an end, the faithful birds with their built-in homing devices have served man long and well. They helped to save lives and win wars. They enabled man to span time and distance. In the annals of the air-mail, they deserve to be remembered. After all, when it comes to delivering mail by air, they can forever claim something that humans cannot. They were first.

A B-18 bomber crew on patrol near Hawaii attaches capsule to pigeon's leg while the pilot folds a message. Note cage on right.

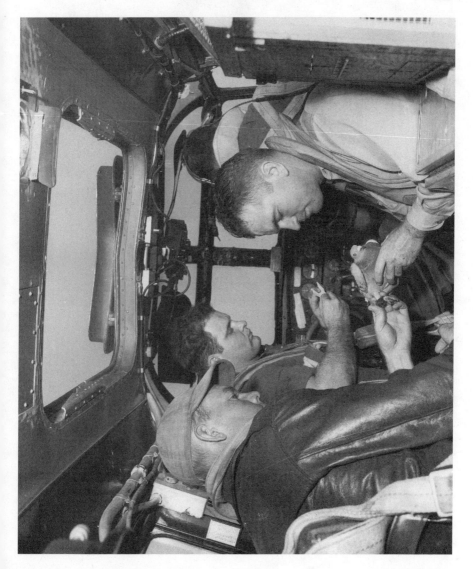

U.S. Navy balloon pilots attach message to pigeon during World War II demonstration.

=== *2* ===

LIGHTER-THAN-AIR MAIL

IN THE YEAR 1784 Pierre Blanchard, a French balloonist, announced that he was going to be the first man in history to fly across the Channel from England to France. Teaming up with an American physician, Dr. John Jeffries, the daring Frenchman readied his hydrogen-filled balloon, to which was attached a bathtub-shaped gondola outfitted with four steering rudders that looked like wings.

On the morning of January 7, 1785, the two ascended from the cliffs at Dover with a light air blowing from the north-north-west. They had stowed various articles of clothing, food, books, musical instruments, and art objects aboard, which almost proved to be too much weight for the balloon to lift. As an after-thought, Blanchard accepted some letters from well-wishers addressed to friends in France. They were wrapped in a pig's bladder to keep them dry.

Dr. Jeffries, in an account published soon after the historic flight, described what happened:

Heaven crowned my utmost wishes with success: I cannot describe to you the magnificence and beauty of our voyage . . . When two-thirds over, we had expanded the whole of our ballast. At about five or six miles from the French coast we were again falling rapidly towards the sea, on which occasion my noble little captain gave orders, and set the example, by beginning to strip our aerial car, first of our silk and finery: this not giving us sufficient release, we cast one wing, then the other; after which I was obliged to unscrew and cast away our moulinet; yet still approaching the sea very fast, and the boats being much alarmed for us, we cast away, first one anchor, then the other, after which my little hero stripped and threw away his coat. On this I was compelled to follow his example. He next cast away his trousers. We put on our cork jackets and were, God knows how, as merry as grigs to think how we should splatter in the water. We had a fixed cord, &c to mount into our upper story; and I believe both of us, as though inspired, felt ourselves confident of success in the event.

Luckily, at this instant we found the mercury beginning to fall in the barometer and we soon ascended much higher than ever before, and made a most beautiful entry into France exactly at three o-clock. We entered rising, and to such a height that the arch we described brought us down just twelve miles into the country, when we descended most tranquilly into the midst of the forest De Felmores, almost as naked as the trees, not an inch of cord or rope left, no anchor or anything to help us, nor a being within several miles. My good little captain begged for all my exertion to stop at the first tree I could reach. I succeeded beyond my comprehension and you would have laughed to see us, each without a coat of any sort, Mr. Blanchard assisting at the valve, and I holding at the top of a lofty tree, and the balloon playing to and fro over us, holding almost too severe a contest for my arms. It took exactly twenty-eight minutes to let out air enough to relieve the balloon without injury. We soon heard the wood surrounded by footmen, horsemen &c and received every possible assistance from them. I was soon well mounted and had a fine gallop of seven miles . . .

One of the pieces of cargo that the two aeronauts did not throw overboard was the packet of letters—the first mail in the world to go by air in a man-made vehicle. The letters were delivered to the addressees with great fanfare by Blanchard himself, as he stressed the fact that he was the first to cross the natural barrier of the sea to deliver written communications between fellow men. The only letter known to have survived is a letter from William Franklin addressed to his son Temple, which has been preserved by the American Philosophical Society. Letters addressed to King Louis XVI, Benjamin Franklin, American's ambassador to France, and the others have been lost.

The fact remains that Blanchard, a Frenchman more interested in personal publicity than personal fortune, had achieved a notable "first" in the history of airmail. He was the world's first aerial mailman and the first to transport letters by air between nations.

After his successful channel crossing, Blanchard decided to come to America to show the nation his skill in this new art. He wanted to become the first man to make an aerial voyage in the United States of America.

Blanchard arrived in the capital city of Philadelphia in December of 1792 and immediately advertised that on January 9, 1793, "at 10 in the morning precisely, weather permitting," he would make a balloon ascension. He chose as his launching place the yard of the Walnut Street Prison because its high walls would prevent damage to his balloon during the inflation and take-off.

He was elated at the reception he received and was determined to "convince the New World that man's ingenuity is not confined to earth alone, but opens to him new and certain roads in the vast expanse of heaven."

At 7:00 A.M., on the appointed day, two cannons began firing a salvo every quarter-hour to remind the populace of the great event. Inside the courtyard a band played lively martial music while the famous aeronaut busied himself around the slowly-expanding varnished silk bag. Dressed in bright blue knee breeches, matching waistcoat, and a large plumed hat, the short, slender daredevil looked like a Shakespearean actor about to enact a great drama. The handsome, self-confident Frenchman was fully aware of the significance of his flight.

At quarter to ten, there was a buzz of excitement outside the prison. A carriage bearing President George Washington arrived. As the dignified Chief Executive stepped down, the crowd hushed respectfully. Fifteen cannons manned by soldiers in full dress uniform roared in salute.

Inside the yard, Blanchard was ready. When the President approached, followed by the French Minister, Blanchard swept off his hat and bowed deeply.

"I am honored, Messieurs," he said. "I only hope that your faith in me will be justified today."

"We, too, are honored, Monsieur Blanchard," President Washington replied in French. "You will make history today just

Balloons with homing pigeons and mail were flown out of Paris during the Siege of 1870. The pigeons returned from outside the city with mail, news, and military information.

No. 64, 1870.

OPEN LETTERS for PARIS.

Transmission of by Carrier Pigeons.

THE Director-General of the French Post Office has informed this Department that a special Despatch, by means of Carrier Pigeons, of correspondence addressed to Paris has been established at Tours, and that such Despatch may be made use of for brief letters, or notes, originating in the United Kingdom, and forwarded by post to Tours.

Persons desirous of availing themselves of this mode of transmission must observe the following conditions:—

Every letter must be posted open, that is, without any cover or envelope, and without any seal, and it must be registered

No letter must consist of more than twenty words, including the address and the signature of the sender; but the name of the addressee, the place of his abode, and the name of the sender—although composed of more than one word - will each be counted as one word only.

No figures must be used; the number of the house of the addressee must be given in words.

Combined words joined together by hyphens or apostrophes will be counted according to the number of words making up the combined word.

The letters must be written entirely in French, in clear, intelligible language. They must relate solely to private affairs, and no political allusion or reference to the War will be permitted.

The charge for these letters is five-pence for every word, and this charge must be prepaid, in addition to the postage of sixpence for a single registered letter addressed to France.

The Director-General of the French Post Office, in notifying this arrangement, has stated that his office cannot guarantee the safe delivery of this correspondence, and will not be in any way responsible for it.

By Command of the Postmaster-General.

GENERAL POST OFFICE,
16th November, 1870.

Printed for Her Majesty's Stationery Office, by W. P. Griffith, Prujean Square, Old Bailey, London, E.C.

Notice posted by the British during the Siege of Paris, 1870.

as you have done in the Old World. May God grant you a safe journey."

As Blanchard climbed into the wicker basket, Washington stepped forward, handed him an envelope, and said, "One more thing, Monsieur. In order to guarantee you safe passage upon completion of your voyage, it would please me if you would take this letter with you."

Blanchard read the letter that the great man had handed him. Although he could not speak English, he could understand the written words. The letter was addressed "To Whom It May Concern" and recommended "to all citizens of the United States, and others, that in his passage, descent, return or journeying elsewhere, they oppose no hindrance to the said Mr. Blanchard; and, on the contrary, they receive and aid him with that humanity and goodwill, which may render to their Country, and justice to an individual so distinguished by his efforts to establish and advance an art, in order to make it useful to mankind in general."

Blanchard thanked the President, and as the artillery battery blasted a final discharge, he threw out some ballast, nodded to his assistants to let go of the restraining ropes, and was lifted gently skyward.

He later wrote in his *Journal of My Forty-Fifth Ascension* the following account of his voyage:

> My ascent was perpendicular and so easy that I had time to enjoy the different impressions which agitated so many sensible and interesting persons, who surrounded the scene of my departure, and to salute them with my flag, which was ornamented on one side with the armoric bearings of the United States, and on the other with the three colors, so dear to the French nation. Accustomed as I long have been, to the pompous scenes of numerous assemblies, yet I could not help being surprised and astonished, when, elevated at a certain height over the city, I turned my eyes towards the immense number of people, which covered the open places, the roofs of the houses, the steeples, the streets and the roads. . . .

The brave aeronaut rose steadily upward. At about "200 fathoms" a strong breeze developed which carried him eastward toward the Delaware River. A flock of pigeons flew by and then scattered wildly, frightened at a human invading their special realm. Over the silvery Delaware, Blanchard leveled off "in a state of perfect equilibrium in the midst of a stagnant fluid."

As the wind began to pick up, and the big balloon drifted rapidly on a southeasterly course across the New Jersey shoreline, Blanchard relaxed briefly and ate a small lunch someone had given him at the last minute and then "strengthened my stomach . . . with a glass of wine." In the distance he thought he saw the Atlantic Ocean through the mist and made preparations to descend. Guiding its downward course carefully by manipulating the gas valve, Blanchard maneuvered the balloon to a safe landing in a plowed field near the town of Woodbury, New Jersey, at 10:56—exactly 46 minutes and 15 miles after his glorious departure from the City of Brotherly Love. The first aerial voyage in America had been brought to a successful conclusion.

Blanchard worked quickly to let the hydrogen out of the silken globe and keep it from dragging across the ground into nearby trees. He quickly unloaded his instruments. With everything properly cared for, Blanchard now had only one problem: how to get back to Philadelphia. He took his compass and sighted back toward the northwest—directly toward the figure of a farmer, pitchfork in hand, staring open-mouthed at the strange man who had just dropped silently from the skies.

Blanchard yelled to the man in French, since he knew no English. This frightened the farmer and he stepped backward several paces. Afraid the man would turn and run, Blanchard held up the letter Washington had given him. The husky farmer, keeping the pitchfork ready to defend himself, approached warily and stared at the letter suspiciously. Blanchard soon discovered that the man could not read English and could not speak French. Although they couldn't converse he did seem to recognize the name "Washington" when the aeronaut spoke that famous name.

A second farmer approached, armed with an ancient musket. Frightened at the sight of the huge silken globe lying limply on its side, he threw down his gun and lifted his hands skyward in prayer. The first farmer emerged from under the folds of the silken bag and explained the situation. Since the second farmer could read the safe-conduct letter Blanchard had no difficulty from that point on.

More people appeared and Blanchard showed them all Washington's letter. The magic name of Washington made an instant impression on these simple folk, and they did all they could to help this flamboyant, intriguing stranger.

Monsieur Blanchard arrived back in Philadelphia that evening by horseback, carriage, and ferry and was greeted by a cheering crowd that formed lines to shake his hand. At 7:00 P.M., he paid his respects to Washington at the Executive Mansion and presented him with the flag he had borne aloft on that epic flight.

The letter from President Washington that Blanchard carried that day has never been found, although its exact wording is known. If it ever is, it will be worth a fortune. Although neither he nor Washington realized it, that letter was the first officially sanctioned airmail letter of all time. It was fitting, perhaps, that America should have his honor. A little over a century later this same country would be the birthplace of the airplane. And it was the airplane that would truly give wings to the mail.

The success of Blanchard in Europe and America encouraged all manner of men to attempt flight in the unpredictable, flimsy gas bags. Rich men, poor men, scientists, teachers, clergymen, kings, and ordinary citizens constructed balloons and soared aloft. The expense and the risk were too much for many, and a few paid with their lives for the exhilarating thrills of ballooning.

But tragedy has never deterred human progress. A few men were able to make a living from the new art of ballooning, and some writers foresaw the balloon as a vehicle of international commerce and mail. "As man goes," they said, "so goes his cargo and his correspondence." Just as with the airplane many years later, however, ballooning had to go through an era of barnstorming. When the novelty of just seeing an ascension began to wear off, people wanted something more exciting. Some barnstormers took to parachuting from their craft, performing high-altitude trapeze acts, making night voyages, or setting records for distance, speed, and altitude. On many of these flights, mail was carried for publicity purposes or to satisfy stamp collectors who were willing to pay a price to have letters in their collections that had been airlifted from place to place.

One of America's first and, perhaps, foremost balloon barnstormers was John Wise. Famous in the middle 1800's, he made several hundred balloon flights and devoted almost all of his adult life to aeronautics. While his admirers believed he was a daredevil who would do anything for publicity, he was really a serious professional who approached his work scientifically. One of his theories was that great currents of air flowed from west to east across the United States. He reasoned that it might be possible to sail a balloon from America to Europe along this river of air and maybe even around the world.

At the age of sixty-one, John Wise prepared to test his theory—not by making the trans-Atlantic flight but, first, by making a trip from St. Louis to New York. If this flight were successful, it was to be followed by the flight across the ocean to the European continent.

On July 1, 1859, four men boarded the *Atlantic*, a strangely beautiful globe, 50 feet in diameter and 60 feet high. It had been constructed by John Lamountane, one of the crew members, and was made of lacquered silk covered by a woven hemp net. Beneath the bag, the net was gathered on an iron load ring to which was suspended a wicker basket. Fifteen feet below the basket a lifeboat, encased in a heavy canvas sling, was attached. A rope ladder enabled the crew to go between the basket and the boat.

A wealthy enthusiast named O.A. Gager had financed Wise's venture and asked to accompany his protégé. Wise agreed and then decided to add Lamountane and a reporter for the St. Louis *Republican* named Hyde to the passenger list. The latter had promised to write a report of the flight, and Wise knew that this publicity would help when it came to financing the trans-Atlantic flight.

The American Express Company, sensing the value of the publicity if Wise were successful, asked if he would carry a few sacks of mail for the United States Express Company in New York. Wise agreed and with each decision to add people, food and mail bags, cut more ballast bags from the basket. At 6:45 P.M., the ground crew cut the restraining lines on Wise's signal, and the crowd cheered. The huge globe, with its double pendant of basket and lifeboat, lifted upward majestically. The four adventurers waved until they could no longer recognize the faces on the ground.

The liftoff had been uneventful, and the quartet of adventurers drifted eastward on a leisurely breeze as darkness enveloped them. During the cold night, the wind shifted and Wise and his passengers drifted northeastward. By dawn they could see Lake Erie through the haze ahead.

"It's breakfast time," Wise announced to his passengers. "Let's drop in on a farm family and pay our respects. Perhaps in return for the pleasure of having us they will offer us a sumptuous feast."

The three passengers heartily agreed and peered over the side as Wise valved out gas for the descent. As the balloon neared the ground, however, Wise was surprised to see that they were traveling at a higher rate of speed than he had ever experienced before. A line dangling over the side caught in some trees and dragged the lifeboat with it. The sudden drag on the balloon basket almost caused the occupants to be pitched overboard.

"Ballast! Ballast!" shouted Wise as he began cutting sand bags loose. The balloon stopped its descent and slowly rose into the calmer air above. The four men heaved sighs of relief, but each realized that a greater danger lay ahead. At 6:45 A.M. they crossed the Lake Erie shoreline near Toledo. The air became turbulent and cumulus clouds formed around them.

"How fast are we moving, Professor?" one of the passengers asked apprehensively.

"It is difficult to say," Wise replied. "But I think we are moving at better than sixty miles an hour."

The quartet of aeronauts floated along uneventfully and by noontime were over Niagara Falls. Wise had dumped more ballast, hoping to rise upward where the wind was more easterly, but he had compounded the problem, for now the clouds surrounded them and they were in a faster stream of wind.

O.A. Gager, who had financed the flight, had made but one previous balloon ascension and was becoming more nervous by the minute. "Professor Wise, I have a suggestion," he said. "I think that is Rochester ahead. Why not descend now and let Hyde and me off? I could take the mail to New York and Hyde could telegraph his story to his paper. You and Lamountane can continue your journey without the burden of our weight."

Wise considered the idea for a moment. "My friend," he said, "do you realize that we are flying at a speed of more than ninety miles an hour? We are descending but we cannot land at this speed. Throw out more ballast!"

The three passengers riding in the lifeboat dangling below Wise in the basket looked around. "There is no more ballast, Professor!" one of them shouted.

"Then throw everything else overboard. We cannot land now!"

The clothes and instruments were tossed unceremoniously over the side. The sacks of mail followed.

For a short time the descent was halted, and the gas bag drifted rapidly northeastward over Lake Ontario. But the relief from the descent was only temporary. Wise could detect that they were getting closer and closer to the tops of the mountainous waves below. He called Gager up from the boat for a conference.

"We are in trouble," Wise announced, with a tremor in his voice. "I think the best course of action is to try to set our craft down in the lake near a boat if we can. Our ballast is gone and we have little left to throw overboard."

Gager did not like this idea. "We should get rid of everything before we try that," he said. "We would surely drown before anyone could fish us out."

Wise nodded. He threw over a valise containing bottles of champagne he had been saving to toast their successful arrival in New York. "I think we should get rid of everything including the boat and get the others up here with us."

Hyde climbed the ladder to the basket while Lamountane stayed behind with an ax. He would chop the double bottom out of the boat first, he said, then cut it loose only as a last resort. He chopped for a few minutes and threw several pieces of wood overboard when the boat smacked the top of a wave. Lamountane was knocked off his feet. He quickly resumed his work, fully realizing now the urgency of his task. Within a few minutes he had hacked enough boards off the boat to cause the balloon to rise several hundred feet. Exhausted, Lamountane joined the others in the wicker basket.

The four apprehensive adventurers fell silent. Suddenly, Hyde spotted a lake steamer, the *Young America*, through the mist. It was crossing directly in their path.

"Shall we set it down and hope they will pick us up?" Wise asked.

"No!" the other three shouted in unison.

"So be it," Wise said. "We should reach the eastern shore of the lake soon. I think the safest thing for us to do is ditch in the water along the beach. As soon as someone sees the shoreline, I will start the descent."

Almost before he could utter the words, Hyde spotted the dark shoreline ahead. Wise immediately reached for the gas valve. He was not quick enough. The balloon was traveling at such speed that it smashed upon the beach violently and bounced upward.

Wise reacted by throwing the grapnel hook out, hoping that it would catch in a tree. It caught but had no effect. The basket smashed and bounced along the tops of the trees and finally slowed down until it came to rest in a tall tree. The gas bag towering overhead tried to continue onward but, anchored by the basket, flopped into another tree and exploded with a loud bang.

The four daring aeronauts were unhurt in spite of the knocking around they had taken. They climbed down and congratulated each other on their good fortune. Within minutes they were surrounded by people who had seen the balloon loom out of the mist along the shoreline and had come running when they saw it go down in the trees near Henderson, New York.

Wise and his companions experienced mixed emotions when they found out where they were. True, they had not landed where they had hoped, and they were glad the flight was over. But they had flown over 1,200 miles and had set a world's record in proving Wise's theory. Wise was secretly elated. But he had one regret. He had thrown the mail pouches overboard and thought that he had not kept faith with those who had paid for the service. However, two days later, the mail pouch washed ashore near Oswego. The mail was undamaged and was eventually delivered to its destination.

Another of the great balloon airmail stories took place in France. The vain, ill-advised Napoleon III, motivated by delusions of grandeur and hoping to restore the lost glories of his famous uncle to the French Empire, had forced a showdown with Germany. Intoxicated with the "Blood and Iron" philosophy of Bismarck, the spike-helmeted Prussian divisions had steam-rollered across the French border toward Paris.

The French had really not yet recovered from the Napoleonic Wars. The Government was not strong, and the French Army was no match for the well-drilled and fully-equipped Prussian divisions. By September, 1870, Paris was surrounded and cut off from the rest of the nation, and the Prussian blockade was so tight that no messengers or spies could get through the Prussian lines.

The French Government, under the leadership of a member of the Chamber of Deputies, Leon Gambetta, and the people of Paris were aroused and became determined not to surrender their capital. But bravery was not enough; other patriots of France had to be rallied to attack the Prussians from the rear and cut them off from their sources of supplies.

One of the first requirements to rally the people was to obtain information about the enemy encircling the city. How were the Prussian troops placed? Were there any areas lightly guarded?

To answer these questions, two balloons were pressed into service. A professional balloonist named Jules Duruof volunteered to fly the first one out and on September 23, 1870, successfully escaped and spread the word to his countrymen. He carried 500 pounds of letters and military documents and proved that the balloon was more than a vehicle to be used only for exhibitions at fairs and carnivals.

The success of Duruof caused Gambetta to call upon Felix Tournochan, an experienced aeronaut, to establish a balloon courier service. M. Tournochan, who preferred to be known by his professional name of M. Nadar, quickly set up two balloon factories and soon a balloon was leaving Paris almost every day for the next two months carrying messages, maps, and pigeons.

Once the project was well established, Nadar volunteered to pilot one of the balloons to carry a particularly important message out. Once safely landed, however, he wanted to do more for his beloved Paris. He announced that he was going to fly *into* Paris and report the progress being made to liberate the city.

Nadar planned to fly from Tours to Paris, a distance of 130 miles. But his task was much different this time. He had to find favorable air currents that would not only carry him that far but enable him to descend in a relatively small area which was encircled by enemy guns.

Nadar waited several days, and then, when he felt the wind was right, he loaded his dispatches and mail aboard, stepped into the small wicker basket, and signalled for the ropes to be cast off at 6:00 in the morning. At first the wind was wrong at a low altitude, so he cast off some ballast and rose to about a mile. He was elated to find that the wind now carried him northeast and by 9:00 A.M. had covered half the distance to Paris. By 11:00 he could see the outskirts of the city and was able to distinguish the Prussian camps below.

When he thought the proper time had come to descend, Nadar released some gas, hoping that he would not release too much and fall short of his goal and into enemy hands. Just when it seemed as though he was going to soar safely over the Prussians' heads, another balloon suddenly appeared drifting toward him. Nadar took out a small French flag and waved it. He was relieved to see the other pilot wave the French tricolor in return. The two balloons, at the same altitude and moving on the same current of air, slowly drifted closer together.

Nadar waved but did not want to yell at the other occupant. He pointed downward to signal that he was going to descend for a landing as soon as he passed over the last Prussian troops below. In answer, the occupant of the other balloon pulled out a Prussian flag with one hand and a pistol with the other. He leaned out over the edge of the basket, took careful aim at the surprised Nadar, and fired. The shot missed, and Nadar whipped out his own weapon and fired several shots. He also missed, but the enemy aeronaut promptly pulled the gas valve and descended rapidly toward the Prussian lines.

Chapter 2

Nadar landed safely in Paris a few minutes later to the cheers of thousands of its citizens. He became a national hero for his feat and has gone down in history as the winner in the world's first air-to-air combat.

History also records that Leon Gambetta himself escaped from Paris by balloon and raised a ragtag army of 156,000 troops to engage the 40,000 Prussians. A cease-fire was arranged in May, 1871, and peace was finally restored.

Altogether, a total of 66 balloons had been successfully launched, of which 58 had landed safely in friendly territory. The amazing total of 2,500,000 letters totaling ten tons were air-lifted. Propaganda leaflets were dropped on the enemy lines, and copies of the first lightweight aerial newspaper, *The Balloon Post*, were carried and distributed throughout unoccupied France.

It is not possible to say that the Prussians were defeated by the ingenuity and courage of the balloonists who braved the elements and enemy bullets to carry their letters and dispatches outside the beleaguered city. However, the fact remains that communications were established which enabled the Parisians to maintain their morale until an army could be mobilized. The Germans were not beaten in the military sense but did cease fighting, and the city was saved from destruction. The balloon that had not been thought to have any value as a carrier of mail had proven to be the only means, other than the pigeon post, that could keep the lines of communication open. From the standpoint of the history of the airmail, the Siege of Paris was the balloon's finest hour.

There were other great balloon flights during which letters were carried. However, these were generally written by well-wishers who sometimes paid for the honor and thus assisted the aeronaut financially. Very few, if any, had the sanction of the Post Office Departments of the countries concerned because delivery to the ultimate destination was not assured.

It is no secret that the overwhelming disadvantage of the free balloon is its inability to be steered against the wind. Some steering mechanism and means of power must be applied. While early balloonists tried sails, paddle wheels and oars, or other devices, they were unsatisfactory. Later aeronauts tried aeolipiles or devices using the reaction generated by a jet of hot air from a steam kettle. Rockets, gunpowder, and even artillery pieces were fired in unsuccessful attempts to provide propulsive force to the balloon in flight. When the steam engine was invented, it, too, was tested. It, too, did not work.

But the desire to overcome the will of the wind remained strong in the minds of men. One of the great moments in aviation history took place on August 9, 1884, when two French Army officers, Charles Renard and Arthur C. Krebs, ascended in an elongated balloon, called a dirigible, which was powered by an electric motor. On that day, they gave the world's first demonstration of an air vehicle that could take off, steer a course into the wind, and return to its starting point under full control.

The electric motor could not develop enough power to propel a dirigible for very long or against a wind above about ten miles per hour. So it remained for a later invention—the gasoline engine—to make the dirigible more practical.

The invention of the Daimler gasoline engine in 1888 not only made automobiles possible but caused renewed interest in lighter-than-air flight. By the turn of the century, many countries saw a new potential for carrying cargo, passengers, and mail as the combination of gasoline engine and gas bag became more successful. Many experimenters were tinkering with nonrigid, semi-rigid, and rigid dirigibles.

The one man who brought the gasoline-engine-powered dirigible to the highest state of the art was Count Ferdinand von Zeppelin, a German, whose name is now synonymous with the giant rigids of the first three decades of the twentieth century. In the summer of 1900, the first rigid dirigible ever built lifted off the waters of Lake Constance with Zeppelin at the controls. The LZ-1 (Luftschiff Zeppelin 1), measuring 420 feet in length and 39 feet in diameter, was powered by two 16-h.p. engines which turned twin four-bladed propellers. A huge rudder was used to control the craft directionally while a sliding weight was used to raise or lower the nose.

The LZ-1 was not successful but was quickly followed by the LZ-2 which had many improvements. While the LZ-1 could only cruise at $8^1/2$ miles per hour, the LZ-2 cruised at 25 miles per hour. The LZ-3 followed and was capable of 38 miles per hour. Though the giant Zeppelins were used as machines of war and 1908 carried 12 people aloft for 12 hours. In the next year, the flight duration had increased to 20 hours. The LZ-5, even bigger and more powerful, flew for 38 hours that same year.

The future for lighter-than-air craft for hauling man and his correspondence never seemed brighter. In 1909 von Zeppelin and Dr. Hugo Eckener created the world's first scheduled airline, Deutsche Luftschiffahrts-Aktien-Gesellschaft (DELAG). Operating from airports in Dresden, Potsdam, Leipzig, Hamburg,

Frankfurt, and Friedrichshafen, DELAG started regular mail and passenger service in 1910 with the *Deutschland I*, a tri-motored dirigible, which accommodated 20 people and 1,000 pounds of mail.

The German airline prospered. Other dirigibles were built, and between 1910 and 1913 DELAG could boast of having made 760 flights totalling nearly 100,000 miles and carried 14,000 passengers without a mishap. By the end of five years of operation, over 37,000 passengers were carried and 3,200 hours of flying time logged—still without a single passenger having been injured or a single letter lost.

DELAG's service ceased as Germany became deeply involved in World War I. Fourteen years lapsed before a war-weakened Germany resumed lighter-than-air passenger and mail service, although the giant Zeppelins were used as machines of war and carried men and dispatches frequently when not being used to bomb English cities.

Under the direction of Dr. Eckener, Germany resumed its leadership of lighter-than-air scheduled operations in the 1920's The *Graf Zeppelin* first flew on September 18, 1928, and until 1937 made mail and passenger carrying flights throughout the world. It made its 100th crossing of the Atlantic in 1935 and had carried 10,400 passengers and tons of international airmail that year.

The *Graf Zeppelin's* success led to the construction of the *Hindenburg*, which was immediately put on the North Atlantic run while the *Graf* was placed on the flight from Germany to Brazil. During the first year of operation, the *Hindenburg* carried 3,530 passengers and 66,000 pounds of cargo and mail.

Although the rigid dirigibles marked the highest state of the lighter-than-air art, the use of motorized gas bags for the transport of people, cargo, and mail was doomed. The success of heavier-than-air flying machines was, of course, a major factor. For all practical purposes, the era came to a close on May 7, 1937, when the *Hindenburg* exploded over Lakehurst, New Jersey. The *Graf Zeppelin* that same day completed its trip to Germany from Rio de Janeiro and never flew again.

The dirigible, filled with highly inflammable hydrogen, was like a flying bomb waiting for a spark to set it off. But even filled with the non-burning helium, the dirigible didn't have a chance for success as an air carrier. It was too big, too slow, too expensive to build, too cumbersome, and too difficult to maintain. It was inevitable that the airplane would replace it as the courier of the clouds.

=== 3 ===

The U.S.
Airmail Begins

DECEMBER 17, 1903, is a milestone in the history of flight. It was on that day that two bicycle mechanics named Orville and Wilbur Wright flew the first powered, controllable, heavier-than-air flying machine. Ironically, few people seemed to notice or care that a pair of brothers, sons of a minister and high school dropouts, had successfully combined the gasoline engine with the glider. Nevertheless, the Wrights persisted in their attempts to improve the machine. They increased the duration, distance, and speed of their flights and improved the control mechanism. Others, seeing what the Wrights had done, imitated and attempted to outdo them, so that by the end of the first decade of the twentieth century individual experimentation was producing a wide variety of aircraft, engines, and propellers. Aviation was at last beginning to touch the practical imagination of many men everywhere.

It was inevitable that the novelty of flying machines would wear off. People wondered what commercial uses could be generated for them. It was inevitable, too, that someone would conceive the idea that flying mail might be possible. And so it was that exhibition mail flights were planned, usually in connection with air shows or fairs. Stamp collectors and "airmail cover" collectors stimulated these exhibitions by their interest, and the letters that have survived the early flights are highly prized today. Usually the planes were only up in the air a few minutes, and the flights were financed by the sale of souvenir post cards or otherwise specially franked or marked envelopes which the public avidly purchased.

Strangely, the first airmail exhibition flight by airplane did not take place in Europe or the United States. On February 18, 1911, at the Indian Arts and Crafts Exhibition at Allahabad, India, an Englishman named Captain Windham gave official birth to the idea. He arranged with the local postal authorities for permission to have a Frenchman, Henri Piquet, fly souvenir cards from the exhibition grounds to Naini, a small town about five miles away. Permission was granted and over 6,000 cards were carried.

Great Britain, France, and Germany were the next countries to authorize exhibition mail flights. At the coronation of George V in August, 1911, the Grahame-White Aviation Company carried an incredible 130,000 cards and letters between London and Windsor Castle.

In the same month pilot Jules Vedrines claimed honors for France by making a postal flight from Issy les Moilineaux to Deauville. German honors went to Josef Hoffman, who carried a bag of copies of the *Berlin Morning Post* from Berlin to Frankfurt, also during August.

In September, 1911, the airmail exhibition fever hit the United States, and for the next seven years airmail exhibition flights took place from one end of the country to the other. All flights were made with the approval of the Postmaster General, without expense to the Government, and in conjunction with some general meeting or fair.

Credit for being the nation's first official airmail pilot goes to Earle L. Ovington. The event was the International Aviation Meet held at Garden City Estates, Long Island, September 23 to October 1, 1911. A temporary post office was built on Nassau Boulevard. Letter boxes were placed at strategic locations around the field where the meet was taking place, and a regular postman made the rounds every hour collecting the letters and taking them to the temporary post office. There the letters were cancelled and placed in an official mail pouch. The pouch was then to be flown to the post office at Mineola, New York, seven miles away. The pilot dropped the pouch to the postmaster on the ground and returned to the airfield.

The Postmaster General, Frank H. Hitchcock, is credited with pushing the idea of a flying machine as a fast, efficient means of transporting mail between two points. At the meet Ovington, flying a cream-colored Bleriot monoplane, the *Dragonfly*, heard of the plan and volunteered his services. He was

The famous 24-cent airmail stamp with inverted center was issued on May 13, 1918 in Washington, D.C. W.T. Robey bought a sheet of 100 of these and sold it for $15,000. Today, a single stamp is worth thousands of dollars.

promptly and formally sworn in at plane-side ceremonies. Although he was to receive no compensation from the Government, Hitchcock felt duty-bound to give him a token payment. He reached in his pocket, fished out a silver dollar, and tossed it to Ovington. "This will make this arrangement official," he said, smiling.

These first flights were not easy for Ovington. There was hardly room for the pilot in the tiny Bleriot, and he had to carry the pouch in his lap. He had arranged for the postmaster to stand out in a field behind the Mineola post office and wave a red flag. On the first flight, he saw the man waving the flag and heaved the sack overboard. As he watched, the sack plopped at the man's feet, broke open, and 649 letters and 1,280 post cards were scattered by the wind over hundreds of acres of countryside. The next day a stronger bag was furnished, and the flights continued without further incident throughout the meet.

Other pilots participating in the Aviation Meet were sworn in as "Airplane Mail Couriers." They were Captain Paul Beck and Lieutenants Henry H. Arnold, T.G. Ellyson, Eugene Ely, Thomas Milling, Edward Hammond, and George Bently. However, there is no evidence that they actually flew the mail. On the fifth day of the Meet, Postmaster General Hitchcock flew with Beck in a Curtiss biplane and intended to drop the mail personally. But the Curtiss could not lift the pilot, passenger, and mail sack. The Postmaster General let Ovington do the job.

In the nine-day period, a total of 32,415 post cards, 3,993 letters, and 1,062 circulars were carried, according to official Post Office Department records.

Ovington's successful airmail flights the next year had so impressed Postmaster General Hitchcock, however, that even before the Aviation Meet was over, he issued an order dated September 30, 1911, as follows:

> The postmaster at New York, N.Y., is hereby authorized to dispatch mails by way of Chicago, Illinois, to the post office at Los Angeles, California, one trip one way by aeroplane service (carrier Earle L. Ovington), provided such mails be carried by a sworn carrier, and without expense to the Department.
>
> Number the route 607001.

The idea for such an authorization had come about as the result of a prize of $50,000 offered by William Randolph Hearst to the first pilot who could fly from coast to coast within thirty days. Ovington had decided to try and planned to do it in a Bleriot Queen monoplane of American make with a 50-h.p. rotary engine designed by a motorcycle company. Neither the plane nor the engine was suited for the job. After several attempts, Ovington gave up.

Another pilot, Robert Forbes, made an unsuccessful start, and he was followed by Calbraith P. Rodgers, a cigar-smoking giant of a man who had been deaf since childhood from a severe case of scarlet fever. Ineligible for military flying, he had learned to fly at the Wright Brothers School at his own expense, had soloed after $1^{1}/_{2}$ hours of instruction, and had bought a Wright biplane.

Rodgers had already set a world endurance record by the summer of 1911 and had won $11,000 in prize money at a Chicago air meet that same year. When Hearst announced the prize for the first coast-to-coast flight, Rodgers arranged for financial backing with J. Ogden Armour, a meat packer, who wanted Rodgers to advertise a new product he was producing—Vin Fiz— a grape-flavored carbonated soft drink.

Rodgers promptly named his Wright plane *The Vin Fiz*

Flyer and agreed to drop leaflets advertising Armour's soda pop along the way. Armour was to pay him $5 per mile and donated a special railroad train to follow him along the route. The preparations were elaborate: the train consisted of three cars—a Pullman for sleeping, a diner, and a combination machine shop, first

Earle L. Ovington, the nation's first airmail pilot, receives mail bag from Postmaster General Frank H. Hitchcock. Ovington flew the *Dragonfly*, a Bleriot monoplane, from Garden City Estates, Long Island to Mineola on September 25, 1911. This was the first official airmail flight in U.S. history.

aid center, and supply room. A total entourage of twenty people tagged along, including Cal's wife and his mother.

As a further source of revenue, Rodgers and his wife had picture post cards printed and advertised them for sale at 25 cents each. They were sold at every take-off point, where the buyers could address them and give them to Rodgers. He would fly them to the next stop and put them into the regular mail system. Each envelope had a privately printed stamp with the notation "Rodgers Aerial Post Vin Fiz Flyer" and a drawing of the airplane. A green one-cent Ben Franklin stamp was used to get the mail through the Government system since Rodgers had no official authorization as Ovington did a few days later at Mineola.

Rodgers left Sheepshead Bay, Brooklyn, New York, on September 17, 1911, amid great fanfare and publicity. His machine was christened, he was kissed by the young girl who did it, and was handed a letter from the Mayor of New York to give to the Mayor of San Francisco. Jamming his goggles down and clamping an unlit cigar between his teeth, Rodgers roared off toward the heart of New York City to drop his first batch of letters. He arrived at Middletown, New York, 105 minutes later.

The next morning Rodgers crashed on take-off, and his plane was damaged so badly that he couldn't get it back in the air for five days. This mishap was minor, however, compared to what happened later. He crashed 16 times in flying the 4,321-mile route to the West Coast. It took him 55 days to make the trip, although he was only in the air for a total of 82 flying hours.

Although he did not qualify for the Hearst prize, his perseverance caught the fancy of the public. His frequent brushes with death, his struggles against the weather, and mechanical failures caused the crowds to get bigger at each stop. He struggled on and was only nine miles from his goal at Long Beach when he crashed for the sixteenth time near Compton. He hit the ground head first, suffered a brain concussion, burns, and a smashed ankle. But a month later, the plucky Rodgers lashed his crutches on the side of the battered *Vin Fiz*, kissed his wife, and flew the last miles to Long Beach.

Cal Rodgers had made the longest flight in history and although he never realized it, he had also carried mail farther by air than any other airman. The letter from the Mayor of New York to the Mayor of San Francisco had survived all the crashes and was with him when he landed on the sandy beach of the Pacific Ocean. For his extraordinary feat of airmanship, he deserves to be remembered in the continuing saga of the airmail.

Major Reuben H. Fleet (left) flew a Curtiss JN6H "Jenny," modified to carry mail, to the Washington, D.C., polo grounds on May 15, 1918. Fleet is shown briefing Lt. George L. Boyle on the route to follow to Philadelphia for the inaugural of the first regularly scheduled airmail service. Boyle became lost soon after takeoff and crash-landed about 20 miles away.

While Cal Rodgers was making history with his transcontinental flight, other pilots were making "first" airmail flights throughout the United States. In St. Louis, Rochester, Atlanta, Savannah, and Wilmington, North Carolina, pioneer airmen Walter R. Brookins, Lincoln Beachey, Hugh Robinson, Beckwith Havens, and Charles F. Walsh flew mail for pay at local carnivals and county fairs before the year 1911 ended.

The United States Post Office Department, recognizing the possibility of developing the airplane into a practicable means of aerial transportation, made recommendations to Congress early in 1912 for an appropriation of $50,000 with which to start an experimental service, but Congress refused to grant the appropriation. In spite of this rebuff, the postal authorities kept up official interest, and during the fiscal year 1912 a total of 31 orders, covering 16 states, was issued permitting mail to be carried on short exhibition and experimental flights between designated points.

Chapter 3

While most of the excursion flights were conducted light-heartedly in a carnival atmosphere, the pilots took their responsibility seriously. Walter R. Brookins, a Wright pilot, was engaged to fly the mail between the post office and the aviation grounds at Altoona, Pennsylvania, on May 18, 1912. He failed to do so and wrote the following letter to Postmaster General Hitchcock:

> It is with sincere regret that I have to report to you that I was unable to carry the mail at Altoona, Pennsylvania, for which you granted me permission. I made one flight there and then narrowly escaped injuring one of the spectators. The grounds were so badly policed that I refused to start my machine again until the spectators were removed to a place of safety. Since that was impossible I considered it wisest not to hazard another flight.
>
> I shall deem it a great honor at any time to illustrate for you the rise of the aeroplane for the postal service and greatly appreciate your kindness to me in the past. Although I have on several occasions carried the mails by aeroplane, the Altoona incident was the first time that I failed to carry out the experiment.

The experimental flights were continued and requests for appropriations were made by the Post Office Department year after year. Finally, during fiscal year 1916, funds were made available for the payment of aeroplane mail service out of the "Steamboat or Other Power Boat Service" appropriation. During that year, advertisements were issued inviting bids for service on one route in Massachusetts and several in Alaska. No bids were received, probably because no suitably constructed planes were available. Nevertheless, negotiations with airplane manufacturers were conducted looking to the earliest possible establishment of an experimental airmail service. The sudden development and improvement of the airplane during World War I and the important role it played as a weapon of war served to strengthen the belief of postal officials that it could be developed into a means of fast mail transportation. Finally, in the fiscal year ending June 30, 1918, Congress appropriated $100,000 for the development of an experimental air route between Washington and New York.

While the Post Office Department had been dickering with the Congress to obtain funds for airmail experimentation in 1916, Mexican bandits, under the leadership of Pancho Villa, had raided the town of Columbus, New Mexico. General John J. Pershing was ordered in pursuit with cavalry troops and America's first and, at that time, only combat Aero Squadron.

The Pershing Punitive Expedition, with its long, tenuous line stretching across the hot sands and mountains from the United States border deep into Chihuahua, afforded the first practical demonstration of the value of aircraft for reconnaissance and mail carrying in American history. Under the leadership of Captain Benjamin D. Foulois, the First Aero Squadron performed magnificently in spite of its ancient equipment. Equipped with eight low-powered Curtiss JN-3 "Jennie" scout planes, the squadron was handicapped by high elevations, vast distances, and the lack of good landing grounds. The Jennies couldn't climb well enough to reconnoiter the mountainous areas where Villa's troops were hiding, while the exceptionally dry climate warped the planes' propellers and the blowing sand wreaked havoc with the engines and fabric. Foulois asked for ten

President and Mrs. Woodrow Wilson wait impatiently for the take-off of the nation's inaugural airmail flight as Postmaster General A.L. Burleson looks on.

President Woodrow Wilson and Major Reuben H. Fleet discuss the upcoming inaugural airmail flight from the Washington Polo Grounds on August 15, 1918, while the plane is being refueled. The president's left hand is bandaged because of burns he suffered from touching a hot gun barrel during a visit to a military unit the day before.

more planes, but there were none to be had. He had no recourse but to use the planes to carry mail and dispatches back and forth between Pershing's ground units.

The First Aero Squadron was only able to use the tired, old Jennies a short time. Six of the eight planes were lost through accidents between March and August, and Foulois was ordered to take the two surviving wrecks back to Columbus where they were destroyed. In spite of the difficulties with the obsolete planes, the air operation was not entirely without success. The First Aero Squadron chalked up a total of 346 hours of flying time on 540 missions covering more than 19,500 miles while performing reconnaissance, photography, and mail-carrying missions.

Foulois eventually received new planes—Curtiss R-2's—and the First Aero Squadron continued its support of Pershing's expedition. During the next few months, more than 3,000 flights were made over the hostile desert sands without a fatality. Many of these flights were made over country in which cavalry and infantry units could not operate. But more important to Pershing and his troops was that the First Aero Squadron began the first regular airmail service on a 110-mile route between Columbus and field headquarters at Colonio Dublan. Planes covered the distance in 66 minutes and never failed to deliver the mail.

The Pershing Expedition officially ended in January, 1917. The rush of world events overshadowed the achievements made and the lessons learned. The Post Office Department does not credit this first airmail service to American troops in Mexico as "official" and historians have ignored the accomplishment altogether. However, the fact remains that pilots of the First Aero Squadron flew official United States mail from one point to another on a regularly scheduled basis without accident and without losing a single letter. To them belongs an accolade that has been denied them for over half a century.

Major Reuben H. Fleet did not care about making history getting an airmail route started. His job as executive officer to Colonel Henry H. "Hap" Arnold in 1918 was to worry about training pilots at 34 fields in the United States. He was concerned with making Army Air Service combat pilots out of plumbers, carpenters, farmers, white collar workers, and college students and getting them to France. His fields didn't have enough barracks, classrooms, tools, instructors, or airplanes; the students were having accidents; and the training planes were underpowered and overworked. Fleet, a broad-shouldered man who would one day be president of his own aircraft company, had enough problems without taking on an unrelated responsibility. Therefore, he was not at all interested or concerned when he read the War Department order dated May 3, 1918, that directed the Air Service to inaugurate an Aerial Mail Service between Washington and New York beginning May 15th.

Late in the afternoon on May 6th, Fleet, hard at work in his office in the War Department Building in downtown Washington, received a summons from Secretary of War Newton D. Baker to come to his office for a conference. " 'Hap' Arnold has recommended you for the job of getting this airmail route started between Washington and New York with stops at Philadelphia," Baker announced bluntly. "The first plane will leave Washington at 11 A.M. on May 15th. President Wilson will be there. Any questions?"

"Mr. Secretary," he said, finally finding the words, "we don't have any airplanes that can fly from Washington to Philadelphia and New York. The best and only plane we have is the Curtiss JN6H and it will fly only an hour and twenty minutes. Its maximum range is 88 miles at a cruising speed of 66 miles per hour."

Baker listened patiently while Fleet explained that the range of a plane was dependent upon its fuel supply, that the "Jennies" had dual controls and were designed to carry only an instructor and student, and that they had no baggage compartment where mail could be stowed. He told of the shortage of pilots, of how very few Air Service pilots had any experience at cross-country flying, how there were no adequate maps available and how good mechanics were almost nonexistent. He would need much more time than eight days to modify some planes, test them, and train some pilots.

"I'm sorry to hear that, Major," Baker answered. "I was under the impression that the Air Service was ready to go. I wish you'd explain to Postmaster General Burleson what you've just told me."

Baker had his secretary phone Burleson to see if he could come over to discuss the mail route. Burleson could, and while he was en route by limousine, Baker suggested that Fleet think of some alternatives, because he felt that the Postmaster General was not the type of man who would understand the difficulties involved in getting airplanes from one point to another on a regular schedule like trains.

By the time Burleson arrived, Fleet had his speech mentally prepared. After Fleet had uttered a few words, Burleson flew into

Major Reuben H. Fleet and Lt. George L. Boyle discuss the length of time the Jenny should take to fly to Philadelphia. The navigational map was a road map. Lt. Boyle, a recent graduate of the Army Air Service flying school, had never flown cross-country before being assigned to fly the mail.

a rage. "What you're trying to tell me, Major, is that the Army can't do the job or you need more time. Is that right?"

Fleet acknowledged that time was the factor since the planes had to be altered to do a job they were not built to do.

"I have already announced to the press that an Army Aerial Mail Service is going to start on May 15th, and it's going to start that day even if your pilots have to land in cow pastures every few miles. And you don't try to tell me the war effort will suffer, either. You just get the mail into the air and don't waste any time telling me your troubles!"

Burleson stomped out and Secretary Baker turned to Fleet and shrugged. "Do the best you can, Fleet. I'll back you all the way."

Fleet knew he didn't have a moment to lose. He immediately called Colonel Edwin A. Deeds, Chief of Air Service Production, and asked him to order six JN6H's from the Curtiss Aeroplane and Motor Corporation at Garden City, Long Island. "Have them leave out the front seat and the front set of controls," Fleet said, "and put a hopper or compartment to carry mail bags up there."

"That sounds easy," Deeds said. "Anything else?"

"Yes. We've got to double the tank capacity for gasoline and oil and we need those ships in eight days."

Deeds whistled but said he would see what Curtiss could do. In the "can-do" spirit that has characterized aviation since its beginning, Glenn Curtiss accepted the order from Deeds. His engineers proposed a simple arrangement of merely doubling and hooking together two 19-gallon gas tanks and two 2$^{1}/_{2}$ gallon oil tanks in tandem.

Fleet telephoned his friend Major August Belmont, owner of the Belmont Park Race Track on Long Island, and asked his permission to use the park for the New York mail terminus so that he wouldn't have to interrupt the training of Army pilots at the Mineola field.

The problem that troubled Fleet most was the acquisition of capable pilots. He needed six and was told to choose four; the Post Office Department would choose the other two.

Fleet chose Lieutenants Howard P. Culver, Torrey H. Webb, Walter Miller, and Stephen Bonsal. The Post Office Department made arrangements with the War Department to have Lieutenants James C. Edgerton and George L. Boyle detailed to airmail duty. Fleet understood why when he learned that Edgerton's father was purchasing agent for the Post Office Department and Boyle's future father-in-law was an Interstate Commerce Commissioner who had "saved the parcel post for the Post Office

Department" against private express companies bidding and fighting the Government in court for the business. Both men had just graduated from primary flying school at Ellington Field, Texas, and had no experience of any kind in flying out of sight of their training field.

Fleet was not at all happy with this information. An experienced pilot himself, he knew that the success of the experiment really lay with the pilots. Even if the planes could be successfully modified and functioned perfectly, it took a human being at the controls to get them from one place to another. His chagrin can be imagined when he was told that Lt. Boyle, the son-in-law-to-be of the hero of the parcel post squabble, would be given the honor of flying the first official airmail out of Washington. Furthermore, the honor of flying the first airmail into the nation's capital was to be given to Lt. Edgerton.

Fleet was furious but was told he had no choice. On May 13, 1918, he took the train to New York with five of the six pilots, having left Boyle in Washington. At the Curtiss factory, mechanics, engineers, and pilots worked around the clock trying to get the planes in shape to fly. By the afternoon of the 14th, only two were ready to go. Leaving Torrey Webb in charge of getting the other four planes ready, Fleet commandeered an ordinary Jenny without extra fuel tanks and assigned it to himself. Edgerton, Culver, and Fleet would fly to Bustleton Field, Philadelphia. Webb would fly from Belmont with the first southbound mail at 11:00 the next morning to Philadelphia, where Edgerton was to fly his pouch on to Washington. Culver would take the mail that Boyle would bring from Washington on to Belmont. Fleet was to fly a modified Jenny to Washington so that Boyle could have the honor the Post Office Department so keenly wanted him to have.

In the late afternoon of the 14th, Fleet took off from the Belmont Park Race Track followed by Edgerton and Culver. He described the flight:

> The weather was frightful; it was so foggy we pilots could not see each other after we left the ground. Even the masts of the boats in the New York harbor were sticking up into the clouds.
>
> I climbed through the fog and came out at 11,000 feet, almost the ceiling of the plane. I flew south guided only by magnetic compass and the sun until I ran out of gas and the engine quit. Since we didn't have 'chutes in those days, there was nothing I could do but ride the Jenny down. I broke out of the clouds at 3,000 feet over lush farm land so I

Chapter 3

just picked out a nice pasture and landed. A surprised farmer sold me a five-gallon milk can of tractor gas but I had trouble getting it in the tank without a funnel. Perhaps three gallons got in the tank and the rest all over me, but darkness was coming and I couldn't wait while he got more from town. I asked him to point out the direction Philadelphia was and took off. Two miles from Bustleton Field I ran out of gas again and landed in a meadow. Since no telephone was available, I persuaded a farmer to drive me to Bustleton Field. Culver and Edgerton had just arrived after similar experiences so I sent Culver with aviation gasoline to get my plane and fly it in.

There were so many things wrong with our planes and their engines that we worked all night to get them in safe flying condition. For example, one gas tank had a large hole in it and we had to plug it up with an ordinary lead pencil. Next morning, one machine was flyable so at 8:40 A.M. I took off for Washington where I landed at 10:35 at the Polo Field in Potomac Park. The mail was due to start twenty-five minutes later.

While Reuben Fleet had been worrying about the technical flying details, another American Army officer, Captain Benjamin B. Lipsner, had been detailed at his own request to the Post Office Department to take care of administrative details. Not a pilot himself, he believed in the idea and had, on his own initiative, volunteered to be the superintendent of operations. On the morning of May 15th, he was waiting nervously at Potomac Park for Fleet to arrive with the first airplane. Although he felt he had solved all the problems at his end, he was worried because President and Mrs. Woodrow Wilson and a number of other important people had been invited to witness the take-off of "the first plane in history to carry mail at an announced time to and from designated places on a regular schedule irrespective of weather."

Lipsner asked himself hundreds of questions as the crowd around the Polo field grew larger. What if something went wrong? Suppose the plane didn't arrive in time? Suppose it didn't arrive at all? If it did come, would it land safely? Would its engine restart? Would the pilot be able to take off over the towering trees at the end of the field? Lipsner shuddered when he thought what the newspapers would say if the experiment failed.

48

The only thought that sustained Lipsner as he scanned the Washington skies was a philosophy that had been born many years before. In 1834, Postmaster General L.T. Barry had written that "the celerity of the mail should always be equal to the most rapid transition of the traveler." If people could go by air safely from place to place, Lipsner reasoned, surely bags of mail could go along. He did not fully understand the problems of the pilots and mechanics who would have to carry out the concept, but he felt that any technical difficulties could always be overcome eventually.

To Lipsner, the plan was simple. When the plane arrived, Lt. Boyle was to leave Washington at 11:00 A.M. for Philadelphia, 128 miles away. He was to pass his bag of mail to Lt. Culver, who was to fly it the remaining 90 miles to Belmont. At 11:00 A.M., while Boyle was en route from Washington, Lt. Webb was to leave Belmont for Philadelphia with the southbound mail. Webb was to turn over his mail pouches to Lt. Edgerton, who would fly them to Washington. The other four pilots were to be kept in reserve and the entire run shared between all six men in order to maintain a six-day-a-week schedule making one round trip per day for three months.

As the minutes ticked by and no plane arrived, Lipsner began to have his doubts. He had an uneasy feeling that something was going to happen. Although the weather was good in Washington, it might be bad along the route from Philadelphia. Since he had heard that some of the mail pilots had just completed flying school and had no cross-country experience, maybe they would get lost.

Sergeant E.F. Waters, one of the mechanics assigned to service the planes at the Washington terminus, saw the look of deep concern on Lipsner's face as he paced nervously back and forth scanning the skies and looking at his watch. "Anything wrong, sir?" Waters asked.

The Captain shook his head. "Not that I know of, Sergeant, but I have a feeling that something's going to go wrong today."

The Sergeant felt the Captain's anxiety, and the two of them strolled silently out to the center of the field. The Polo Grounds had never been intended to be a landing field, but it was the only open flat space available in the City of Washington at the time. Towering trees stood like sentinels around the field. The flimsy fabric and wood Jennies had been flown from there on demonstration flights before, but. . . .

"Has anybody ever hit those trees on take-off, Sergeant?" the Captain asked, pointing toward the end of the field.

Chapter 3

"Not yet, sir," Waters replied quietly. But both men knew there might be a first time and it could be that day.

As the two walked toward a small temporary hangar, they noticed the crowd had gotten larger. Soldiers had been sent from nearby Fort McNair and stationed around to keep the crowd off the field. A touring car drove up and several policemen got out. Lipsner glanced at his watch nervously. It was 10:30 and the plane that was to make the first flight hadn't arrived yet!

"Where *is* that plane?" Lipsner asked the sergeant. Waters shrugged. There was nothing either of them could do. Army planes didn't carry radios. Major Reuben Fleet, the pilot ferrying the plane, had no way of telling anyone where he was.

As Lipsner paced back and forth, he was approached by a Secret Service agent who wanted to know exactly where the incoming plane would be parked and how it would take off. This was the first inkling Lipsner had that the President was definitely going to come. The Postmaster General had extended the invitation, but Lipsner had never been told whether or not the President had accepted.

"Now we know President Wilson is coming," Lipsner whispered to the sergeant, "but what about Major Fleet? And where is Lt. Boyle?"

Waters could only shrug again in despair. Was Major Fleet going to make it on time or would his Captain have to apologize profusely to their Commander in Chief, the Postmaster General, and the press?

Lipsner kept looking at his watch and peering anxiously skyward. Suddenly, above the buzz of the growing crowd, Lipsner heard the most welcome sound of his life. It was the unmistakable engine and prop noise of the Jenny!

Major Fleet circled the field once and landed. He taxied to the hangar and shut off the engine. His face broke into a big grin.

"Were you worried about me?" he asked Lipsner, whose face still wore a king-sized frown.

"You bet I was," Lipsner retorted. "And I still am, because Lt. Boyle isn't here yet. If he doesn't show up, will you make the first mail run? The President is due here in a few minutes."

"That won't be necessary, Captain," a voice spoke from the corner of the hangar. "Never fear because Boyle is here." Behind him was his financee, Miss Margaret McChord, grinning sheepishly and holding an armful of red roses.

Neither Fleet nor Lipsner smiled at the remark. Both felt that their respective military careers hung on Boyle's performance.

Major Fleet climbed out of the cockpit, reached down, and undid the road map he had strapped to his thigh. He handed it to Boyle. "Here, Boyle, I'll show you how to get to Philly," he said casually.

A few minutes after Fleet arrived, a line of shiny black cars chugged into the entrance to the Polo Grounds. Men were standing on the running boards and jumped off one by one as the cars pulled up beside the plane. President and Mrs. Wilson stepped down from the lead car smiling. Just as the President shook hands with the two pilots, a siren sounded across the field, and a motorcycle escort sped ahead of a mail truck. The truck braked to a stop on the edge of the crowd and was quickly unloaded.

The crowd pressed closer. As the Washington postmaster, Merritt Chance, held one of the mail bags open, President Wilson dropped in a letter addressed to Postmaster Thomas G. Patten in New York City. The President had written his name across the stamp.

Fleet stood on the sidelines watching the ceremonies and assumed that Lipsner's men were taking care of servicing the Jenny. When the formalities were completed and the bags placed in the plane, Lt. Boyle strapped himself in the cockpit. "Switch off!" he shouted to Sergeant Waters. Waters twisted the propeller around three times.

"Contact!" Waters yelled, and Boyle answered, "Contact!" Boyle turned the switch on and Waters put all his weight on the propeller to spin it into life. The engine coughed once and died. A puff of smoke blew out of the engine exhaust and disappeared. Waters tried again. The engine coughed again and died.

Waters tried again and again until beads of perspiration stood out on his reddening forehead. Fleet, standing on the sidelines, quickly thought over the many reasons why an airplane engine wouldn't restart when it had acted so well only a few minutes before. He ordered Waters to check the spark plugs. Nothing wrong there.

Fleet ran up to the plane and checked the gasoline gauge. It showed full. What else could it be? Behind him he heard the President whisper to Mrs. Wilson, "We're losing a lot of valuable time here."

Suddenly, Fleet thought he knew what the trouble was. "Sergeant, check the gas tank," he ordered. He knew that the gas gauges were often completely unreliable.

Waters climbed up on the plane's wing and took off the gas tank cap. He stuck a stick inside the tank, probably knowing what he would find. He pulled the stick out dry and shook his head. Fleet rushed over to a British plane parked nearby and immediately filled a gas can. He hurried back to Boyle's plane and handed it to the Sergeant. "Pour it in quickly," he said.

When the can was empty, Waters dipped a stick inside the tank. Only about a third of it was wet when he pulled it out. The tank had been almost empty. In the excitement of the arrival of the President, the formalities and the picture taking, everything had been checked but the gas tank!

Waters finished filling the tank and assumed his place in front of the plane. He spun the prop, and this time the engine roared into life immediately. Everyone, including the President, smiled with relief.

Lt. Boyle tested the controls, raised his arm as a signal for the chocks to be pulled away from the wheels, and taxied a short distance from the crowd. Turning into the wind, he pushed the throttle forward and blasted off toward the trees at the far end of the field.

Bumping stiffly on its tail skid at first, the frail flying machine slowly gathered speed and lifted smoothly into the air. Leveling off slightly, Boyle gained additional flying speed. But he was heading straight for the trees!

The crowd gasped and fell silent. At the last second, Boyle eased back on the stick and sailed skyward, missing the top branches by all of three feet. As he disappeared beyond the trees, the crowd breathed a deep sigh. The nation's first official airmail was in the air and on its way.

As the President and his party climbed into their cars, the crowd slowly drifted away, photographers closed up their cameras, and reporters folded their notebooks. Everything had gone just as the Post Office Department had said it would in the press releases. Fleet was invited to the White House were the President presented him with a wrist watch to commemorate the occasion.

Lipsner was aware that the crowd was leaving, but he couldn't take his eyes from the sky. Boyle had taken off to the north toward Philadelphia, but from the sound of his engine he was turning in the opposite direction. Was he coming around for a landing or was he, like a homing pigeon, going to get his bearings first before he headed back toward his destination? Or was he just plain lost?

Lipsner was helpless with frustration. Without a radio there was nothing he could do to tell Boyle about his mistake. He looked hurriedly around him, but no one else seemed to realize what was happening. Fleet had already gone, and he was left alone with his agonizing knowledge. Maybe Boyle would soon realize he was off course and eventually turn back. Or maybe he wouldn't.

Completely dejected, Lipsner walked slowly back to his temporary office in the Post Office Building. There was nothing he could do but wait for the telephone to ring and hope that the President, the Postmaster General, and the press wouldn't hear about what happened before he did.

No sooner was he seated at his desk than the phone did ring. It was a call from New York telling him that Lt. Webb had taken off exactly on schedule. That made Lipsner feel better, but what if Webb got lost too?

Later, the phone rang again. It was Philadelphia calling. Webb had landed there and turned over his pouch to Lt. Edgerton. Edgerton had immediately taken off for Washington. The next time that phone rings, Lipsner thought, it had better be someone saying that Boyle had landed in Philadelphia.

A call finally did come from Boyle about an hour later. "Captain, I'm sorry to have to tell you this," he said with embarrassment, "but my compass got a little mixed up and I got lost."

"Where are you, anyhow?" Lipsner demanded.

"I'm down here at Waldorf, Maryland," was the answer. "I had to set the Jenny down in a farmer's field because I was running out of gas."

"What about the mail?" Lipsner asked curtly.

"It's being put into a mail truck right now and will be taken back to Washington. And, Captain, . . ."

"Yes?"

"I almost forgot. The airplane went over on its back when I landed and damaged the prop. It'll take a while to fix."

Lipsner was furious, but there was nothing he could do. After an hour of flying, Boyle had ended his flight only 20 miles southeast of Washington. The young lieutenant, unhappily, had become not only the first official airmail pilot, but also had the dubious honor of being the first one to get lost and the first to have an accident.

Boyle's mail bags were sent to New York the next day by air. They contained 6,600 letters, including the one President Wilson had cancelled with his signature. (This letter was auctioned off for the Red Cross at the Collectors Club in New York City. It was purchased by Noah Taussig for the $1,000 minimum bid price and is now possessed by his son, president of the American Molasses Company.)

Fortunately for Lipsner and the other men who believed in

the airmail, the first day of the experiment was termed a success by the nation's press. The papers were too full of war news to bother about Lt. Boyle's mishap. Lt. Edgerton landed at the Polo Grounds on schedule that afternoon as did Lt. Harry Culver at Belmont, even though he had no Washington mail to deliver to New York.

While no one else seemed to worry about Boyle's flying skill, Fleet was very concerned. He wanted a replacement pilot, but the Post Office Department asked that Boyle be given a second chance. Two days later, Boyle took off again, this time with Fleet flying ahead in a training Jenny to make sure he got well along on the right compass course. About forty miles north of Washington, Fleet cut his throttle and yelled at Boyle.

"Are you O.K.?" he asked the young lieutenant.

Boyle waved and yelled back confidently, "I'm O.K., Major."

Thus reassured, Fleet peeled off and returned to Washington. An hour later, Boyle became lost and landed in a pasture near the mouth of Chesapeake Bay. He quickly obtained some tractor gas from a farmer and took off again. Once more he became disoriented, ran out of gas, and crashed near the Philadelphia Country Club, only a few miles from his destination. The wing of his plane was smashed to splinters, but Boyle was unhurt. His mail was once more trucked to a take-off point.

To Fleet's dismay, the Post Office Department again requested that "Lieutenant Boyle be given a third chance and, if he fails, the Department will take responsibility for his failure." Fleet denied the request and was backed up by Secretary Baker.

Lt. Jim Edgerton, the other Post Office Department selectee, had none of the difficulties Boyle had in navigating. He served during the entire experiment without accident. But, in retrospect, Reuben Fleet does not believe that George Boyle should be criticized in the hindsight of a half-century. He told the author:

> There were no maps of much value to airmen in those days. Major E. Lester Jones, Chief of the Geodetic Survey Office, made up maps for the airmail pilots. The official state maps of New York, New Jersey, Pennsylvania, Delaware, and Maryland were all of different scales and they showed only political divisions with nothing of a physical nature except cities, towns, rivers, harbors, etc. We had to fold large maps of the United States in a strip in order to have everything on a uniform scale. Naturally, these contained little detail.
>
> In addition to poor maps, the magnetic compass in any

airplane was highly inaccurate and was affected by everything metal on the airplane. Pilots had to almost have a
sixth sense about navigating and many didn't acquire this
until they had flown a long time. Lt. Boyle simply didn't
have enough training to do the job and should not be criticized too severely for his mistakes.

Fortunately for Fleet, Lipsner, Boyle, and the Army Air Service, Boyle's mishaps did not receive any attention in the press.
Instead, a bigger story broke in connection with the inauguration of the airmail that still arouses attention from magazine
and newspaper writers. It concerns the case of "The 24¢ Air Mail
Inverted Center of 1918."

The story began with a routine Post Office press release stating that new 24-cent airmail postage stamps would be issued in
Washington on May 13, 1918, and the next day in Philadelphia
and New York and would be available for use in connection with
the first and subsequent airmail flights. W.T. Robey, an ardent
stamp collector, went to the window of the Post Office located on
New York Avenue in downtown Washington and was issued a full
sheet of 100 of the new stamps for which he had just withdrawn
money from his savings account. Robey took one look as the
clerk slid the sheet toward him "and my heart stood still." For a
stamp collector he was experiencing the thrill of a lifetime. The
entire sheet of stamps had the engraving of the airplane *upside
down!*

Without comment, Robey paid for the sheets and left. He
made attempts later in the day to find similar sheets in other
branch post offices but was unsuccessful. No other such sheet
was ever printed. His inquiries, however, caused him to be vis-
ited by postal inspectors who offered him a sheet of "good"
stamps for his sheet of inverts. Robey refused. He knew he had a
valuable find, and there was no law that said he had to give his
sheet back. The only thing that he didn't know was just how
valuable his acquisition was.

Robey went to New York and made the rounds of the stamp
collectors. He received offers varying from $2,500 to $15,000 for
the entire sheet and finally sold it for the latter figure to Eugene
Klein of Philadelphia for a profit of $14,976.

The sheet of 100 stamps was eventually broken up and
today the whereabouts of only 81 of the stamps is known. The
value of each of these stamps had escalated over the years. A
block of four (there are seven of these known to exist), which is
the largest multiple of this stamp, was recently purchased for

the record sum of $100,000. Single stamps have been sold for more than $4,000 each.

As with priceless paintings, money, and other man-made items that have a high value, counterfeiters have made copies of this famous philatelic mistake. Stamp dealers and collectors, however, are wary of such efforts and have been able to spot these fakes so far without difficulty.

The Post Office Department did not enjoy the publicity given their most notorious printing error. The remaining sheets in the three post offices were called in and the printing plate was altered so that the word "top" was added for the benefit of the printers, who had to run the stamp through both a red and blue printing. Only a limited printing of this stamp was ever made. In July, 1918, the price of the stamp was lowered to 16 cents and a green stamp was issued. In December, a six-cent orange stamp was issued as the airmail postage was further lowered.

While the stamps commemorating the first experimental airmail caused more attention than the flights themselves, the Air Service pilots proved that they could maintain regular schedules in spite of the risks which only they knew or understood. Mail *could* be moved by air from one place to another on schedule if a proper system were set up, the airplanes properly maintained, and the pilots trained.

On August 12, 1918, the airmail experiment ended. The Post Office Department bought its own planes, hired its own pilots, and continued the airmail service. Captain Ben Lipsner stayed on the job directing the operation until he was permitted to resign. When he was released from the Army, he became the first man to hold the title of "Superintendent of the United States Aerial Mail Service."

The Army Air Service had added another "first" to its credit while attempting to build an air force to fight the war in Europe. The airmail was an unplanned sideline which had to be undertaken in a hurry, without adequate time to prepare for the task. Twenty-six years later it was destined to fly the mails again but with even less warning and with tragic results.

From the point of view of philately, the hobby of stamp collecting, the original 24-cent airmail stamp of 1918 is the outstanding airmail stamp of all time. Not only was it the first definitive air stamp of the world, but it was the first showing an airplane, the first to be printed in two colors, and the first to be printed with a mistake.*

*Italy issued airmail stamps in 1917 and Austria in 1918, but these issues were "provisional" and not "definitive." Neither was used with or based upon a regularly scheduled airmail service.

=4=

THE GLORY YEARS

THE PIONEER ARMY AIR SERVICE pilots continued to fly the New York–Washington, D.C., route between May 15 and August 12, 1918, without much public notice. Although few people knew it, the pilots still had their difficulties. The pledge to keep on a regular schedule six days a week caused the pilots to take exceptional risks. Forced landings due to mechanical difficulties were frequent, but the greatest threat was the weather, for bad weather, then as now, was the natural enemy of the flier.

As far as can be determined, Lieutenant James C. Edgerton, pilot on the Philadelphia to Washington run on the first day, was the first pilot to fly through a thunderstorm while carrying mail. In July, 1918, on his regular route out of Philadelphia for the nation's capital, he saw an ever-darkening sky in front of him. Lightning flashed and angry clouds boiled upward to blot out the sun.

Edgerton had a choice. He could turn back and land in a smooth field while he could still see and the air was relatively quiet, or he could stay on course and see what thunderstorms really would do to an airplane. He looked at his watch and elected to stay on course.

First a little turbulence struck the fragile Jenny and caused it to buck and pitch, but not so violently that it couldn't be controlled. Then the air turned cool and the rain began, light at first, and then drenching the pilot.

Edgerton recalled afterward that when he hit the middle of the storm area, he felt as though he had hit a stone wall. He had no visual references to keep his plane steady, and the pitching became so violent that he could hardly keep the stick in his hand. The severe jolts the plane received made Edgerton doubt that the wings would stay on. When hail began blasting the plane it was as though a million bullets were striking the skin-tight fabric covering the plane's wooden skeleton.

It seemed to Edgerton that he was at the mercy of the giant thunderstorm for an hour, but it was actually only a few minutes. When he emerged into the sunlight on the other side, he found he was still on course and still had full control of the Jenny. After landing at Potomac Park, however, he found that the hail had splintered the wooden propeller. Strangely, there were no tears in the fabric, and no weakening of the wooden structure was found in spite of the vicious jolts the plane had taken.

By just such encounters with the weather, pilots gradually overcame their fear of bad weather while, at the same time, developing a healthy respect for their own physical limitations and the limitations of their planes. They were like sailors traversing unchartered oceans in ships of unknown seaworthiness. The airmail pilots chartered their oceans aloft and found that their winged ships were capable of doing the job asked of them.

When the airmail experiment ended on August 12th, the statistics of accomplishment were impressive. The Army pilots had successfully completed 92 percent of their scheduled flights and had carried 193,021 pounds of mail. They had flown a total of 128,255 route miles without a fatality. The problems they had faced, however, were also reflected in their reports. They had flown a total of 1,208 flights out of a scheduled 1,263. The difference of 55 flights was due to cancellations caused by bad weather or unavailability of flyable planes. Of the trips flown, 53 were forced down because of bad weather en route and 37 ended in forced landings due to mechanical difficulties.

The man responsible for organizing and running the airmail experiment for the Army was Captain Benjamin B. Lipsner. He had kept accurate records and had organized the system so well that Otto Praeger, the second assistant Postmaster General, asked Lipsner to continue running the airmail for the Post Office Department. "You made it work for the Army, Ben," Praeger said. "Now I want you to run it for us. Airmail is here to stay and we've got plans to expand the service clear across the country."

Lipsner was flattered to have been asked to stay on, but there were some technicalities to be ironed out. He was still in uniform and there was a war on. Besides, he wanted to go to

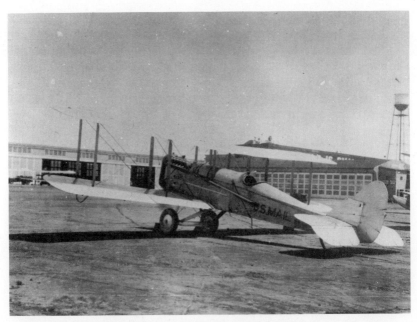

De Havilland trainers were used by civilian pilots of the U.S. Post Office Air Mail Service between 1918 and 1927. Private companies were given contracts beginning in 1925, marking the start of the commercial airline industry in the United States.

France where almost all of the officers he had known in the service had already been sent.

Praeger was a man used to untangling red tape and a great persuader. He wrote to Secretary of War Newton D. Baker asking that Lipsner be granted a leave of absence, but this request was denied. Instead, Lipsner was permitted to resign in order to accept the job as the first Superintendent of the Aerial Mail Service. On July 15, 1918, before the Army experiment was actually completed, he accepted this newly created post. He immediately requested that six specially-built mail planes be completed and made arrangements to have a completely civilian staff by the time the Army completed the 90-day trial period.

The switchover from military to civilian operation was not easy. Most aircraft mechanics and pilots were still in uniform. Furthermore, Lipsner did not find many people inside the Post Office Department as enthusiastic about the idea of flying the mail as Praeger was. The first three months of operation had not been profitable after the initial flights because only stamp collectors seemed to be interested in sending letters between Washington and New York. Not enough time was saved only this relatively short distance, which was also served by fast trains. To be profitable and worthwhile, airplanes had to span greater distances and run between the large centers of population across the country. This need, early realized by Lipsner and his superiors, was the genesis of the idea of transcontinental airmail.

The planes Lipsner chose were among the first in the world to begin with specifications that sprang from the job to be done. Working with engineers of the Standard Aircraft Company of Elizabeth, New Jersey, he set the load specifications at 180 pounds of mail. The plane had to have a speed of 100 miles per hour and the capability of climbing to 6,000 feet in 10 minutes. The Standard Aero-mail plane was born, powered by a 150-h.p. Hispano-Suiza engine. Six were ordered and they were accepted by the Government a week before the Army was to finish its three-month experiment. The first government commercial aircraft was thus successfully completed, and the acceptance ceremony marked the birth of commercial aviation in the United States. On August 12, 1918, the first civilian commercial airmail flights were successfully completed. A new era had begun.

Ben Lipsner was a visionary who foresaw the country crisscrossed with "airways" or air routes which would connect the major population centers and enable anyone to send mail by air to anyone else in another city and have it arrive sooner than by any other means. A route was laid out from New York to Cleveland which was to be the first step in a transcontinental airway stretching the 2,600 miles from New York to San Francisco. Named the Woodrow Wilson Airway, it was 80 miles wide—40 miles on either side of the center line "so that the air traveler of that day could reach the extreme part of either side of the zone in a half-hour of flying." Similar smaller airways fed into the Wilson Airway and were named after leaders in aviation of that day.

Exactly one year after the official beginning of the airmail, the New York – Cleveland schedule began. On September 5, 1919, the route was stretched to Chicago as Max Miller and Ed Gardner, the first civilian airmail pilots hired, raced each other from New York to see who would land in Chicago first. Miller won.

On May 15, 1920, the third leg of the transcontinental route was extended from Chicago to Omaha. On August 16th a route was established between Chicago and St. Louis, and on December 1st of that same year another route was established between Chicago and Minneapolis.

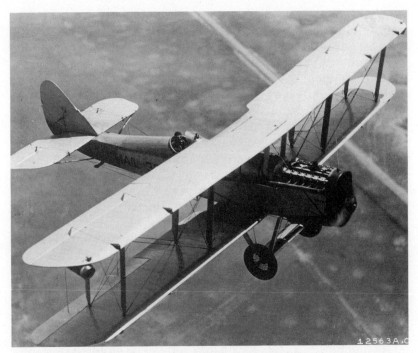

A view of a de Havilland mail plane in flight. Note the landing light for night operations on the right wing tip.

The last leg of the transcontinental route from Omaha to San Francisco via North Platte, Nebraska; Cheyenne, Rawlins, and Rock Springs, Wyoming; Salt Lake City, Utah; and Elko and Reno, Nevada, was inaugurated on September 8, 1920. The initial westbound trip was made at an average speed of 80 miles per hour and was flown without a single forced landing either for weather or mechanical trouble. The first plane carried 16,000 letters and arrived in San Francisco 22 hours ahead of the best train time.

The airmail operation up to 1921 was strictly a daytime operation and was performed in coordination with the railway trains. Mail was carried by airplane only during daylight hours from station to station across the established routes. During the night the mail continued its forward movement in the railway mail cars. The next logical step, once the route extended from coast to coast, was to see if mail could be flown at night.

The experiment was scheduled for February 22, 1921— Washington's birthday. That morning, two pilots left San Francisco and two left New York carrying 350 pounds of mail and flying DH-4's powered by Liberty engines. It was hoped that one set of pilots would succeed in getting the mail through in less than 36 hours.

Pilots E.C. Leonard and Ernest Allison took off from Hazelhurst Field on Long Island a few minutes apart. On the West Coast, Pilots Farr Nutter and W.F. Lewis left San Francisco before dawn and headed east. Within a few hours, tragedy overtook the eastbound flight. Lewis, taking off from Elko, Nevada, for Salt Lake City, stalled while climbing and crashed. By the time the ground crew could get to him, he was dead.

On the westbound run, Leonard was forced down because of the weather. Allison, meanwhile, had transferred his mail to Wesley L. Smith, who sped on toward Chicago.

Farr Nutter turned his mail over to Jack Eaton at Reno who, in turn, flew the pouches to Salt Lake City, where he was relieved by J.P. Murray. Murray raced on to Cheyenne and flipped his bags into the mail compartment of Frank Yager's plane. Yager flew on to North Platte, Nebraska, where he gave his bags to Jack Knight.

Fifteen hours had now elapsed, but the toughest part was yet to come. Word had been sent that the single westbound plane had gotten as far as Chicago, only to be stopped by winter weather. A cold front bringing a nasty blizzard was on the way. It would be suicide to try to continue westward.

But could the eastbound mail continue? If a pilot couldn't take off from Chicago, could a pilot land? The ground crews thought not and all went to bed.

At North Platte, darkness obscured the familiar landmarks around the flying field. Jack Knight shivered as he fastened his seat belt and started the engine. He took off and headed east toward Omaha, unaware that the success or failure of this first attempt at day-night operation would lie on his shoulders.

Because there were few lights along his course, Knight found it difficult to navigate. To make matters worse, a layer of clouds at 2,000 feet covered the sky, the blackness obscured the horizon and made it difficult to keep the wings level, and visibility ahead was being cut down by mist.

Faithfully following his magnetic compass and verifying his position by the occasional lights he could see on the ranches below, Knight kept on. His attempt had been publicized in the papers and, although he didn't realize it, hundreds of people below him were listening for the hum of his Liberty engine. At Lexington, Kearney, and Central City, along the Platte River, he found that people had lit huge bonfires to cheer him on and to assure him that he was on course.

Although it was after 1 A.M. when he neared Omaha, Knight was surprised to find the entire city lit up. It seemed that everyone in town had turned on his lights to welcome him. He landed with the aid of blazing drums of gasoline around the field, taxied up to the operations shack, and leaped out. The 276-mile flight had wearied him, and his eyes stung from peering through the blackness. He was glad his part in the inaugural flight was over.

Strangely, the ground crew was glum and unsmiling. Knight asked one of them what was the matter.

"You'll find out inside, Jack," he was told. "Looks like this first try at getting the mail through coast to coast is a bust."

Inside the operations office, Knight learned that the pilot who was to meet him and take his pouches to Chicago was weathered in at the Windy City. He pulled off his gloves and warmed himself by the wood stove. The station manager, Bill Votaw, helped him out of his leather flying jacket.

All types of aircraft were used to carry the mail to and from U.S. troops in the overseas combat theaters during World War II. Here mail bags are loaded aboard a Consolidated B-24 bomber.

Chapter 4

"Bill, it seems a shame to have to quit this flight when we've gotten the mail halfway," Knight said. "Let me get warmed up here a few minutes and I'll take 'er on through to Chicago."

"Jack, don't kid me," Votaw retorted. "You've never flown the Omaha-Chicago route. Even in daylight you'd never make it in this kind of weather."

"If people will keep lighting bonfires, I can make it," Knight answered. "All I need is some of your good coffee and I'll give it a go."

Votaw shrugged. He had no authority to prevent a pilot from taking off. All he could do was give the pilot every assistance on the ground. The final decision to go or not rested with the pilot.

The weather reports along the 435 miles to Chicago were discouraging. Snow showers were predicted over the entire route, which meant zero-zero conditions wherever snow was falling.

"How about a map?" Knight asked. "Got to have a map."

"Sorry, old man," Votaw replied. "The only map we've got is our Rand-McNally road map on the wall."

Knight sipped his coffee and studied the map carefully. He reached up and ripped off the section between Omaha and Chicago and put it in his pocket.

"Spread the word I'm coming, Bill, and wire my wife," he said, buttoning up his jacket. A few minutes later he pointed the nose of his DH-4 eastward toward Des Moines.

Outside of Omaha the clouds thinned and Knight broke into the clear. He wondered how long it would last.

The lights of Des Moines were visible when he was about 30 miles out, but the weather reports bothered him. If he landed, time would be wasted on the ground, so he decided to push on through to Iowa City. But a few miles east of Des Moines he noticed that his view of the ground was being cut off by a sheet of cloud. He nosed down to get below it, knowing that if he could not see landmarks that he could identify from the piece of road map he had, his chances of getting to Iowa City and then to Chicago were nil.

Below the clouds, at 1,000 feet, the air was bumpy. Snow began to pelt him in the face. Visibility was reduced to about two miles, and gradually Knight lost his horizon. To make matters worse, he began drifting to the right of course as the northerly winds increased. His ground speed was reduced to 80 miles an hour, and he began to wonder if his gas would hold out. Since he had passed up the gas stop at Des Moines, he wouldn't have

64

Mail and small packages were carried aboard this L-5 liaison plane in New Guinea during World War II.

much to spare even if there were no head winds to slow him down. He decided to press on.

The fluffy white ceiling above him descended slowly, and he was forced to descend with it. The landmarks were more difficult to see now, and he found it nearly impossible to compare the things he saw on the ground with the printed symbols on the map. Every time he switched on his flashlight he was temporarily blinded, so he decided to navigate by memory. He would follow the railroad as long as he could identify it.

Knight's DH-4 bumped and chugged along while its pilot strained right and left to see what was ahead. Iowa City had to show up soon.

Almost as a surprise, Knight found that he had flown right over the center of Iowa City. But where was the airport? It didn't show on the map, and he had forgotten to ask where it was in relation to the town before he took off.

Knight flew around and around the sleepy city, gunning his engine. Ten minutes later, he saw the welcome glow of a red flare which had been lit by the night watchman at the airport. The ground crew, hearing that the westbound flight had been cancelled, had left the airport and gone home.

Chapter 4

Knight bumped to a landing and taxied up to the lone figure holding a lantern. Just as he was about to cut the switch, the engine quit from fuel exhaustion. Tired, numb with cold, and irritated that the word of his coming had not gotten through, he stumbled to the operations building and flopped into a chair near the fire. A few minutes later the ground crew, awakened by his low passes over the city, arrived and serviced his plane. It was now about 5 A.M. and he still had 200 miles to go. He dozed for five minutes and awakened with a start. He leaped up, buttoned his jacket, drew on his gloves, and rushed out the door. Once more, he would "give it a go."

As soon as Knight leveled off under the clouds, which were now about 500 feet, he noticed it was getting light. Down below he could see farmers with lanterns going about their morning chores. "Only farmers and mail flyers are up at this ungodly hour," he mused.

Knight's eyes burned behind his goggles. He found it difficult to focus on his compass and the map, to stay awake. He was aware that his reactions were slow, but he knew he had to stay awake, especially at such a low altitude. He devised ways to overcome the drowsiness, like moving his goggles up on his forehead and letting the cold air wash his burning eyes, or stretching his arms out into the slipstream and his legs past the rudder pedals to stimulate his circulation.

The plane droned on. Light snow turned to sleet, and the danger of ice forming on the wings stirred Knight wide awake. Visibility was poor, but the coming of daylight enabled him to see the parallel tracks of the railroad pointing eastward to Chicago.

The official Post Office records show that airmail pilot James H. "Jack" Knight arrived at Maywood Airport in Chicago at 8:40 A.M. on February 23, 1921. They do not show that he received a tumultuous welcome by the people of Chicago and was hailed as "the ace of the airmail service." For two days the nation's papers carried the story of Knight's feat in bold headlines. Every word he uttered to reporters appeared in print in the next editions. This hazardous flight of one pilot who had faced both the elements and the difficulties of night flying caught the public's fancy as nothing had since World War I. The modest Knight had become a national hero.

While public attention was focused on the skinny, tired lad, his mail was whisked eastward from Chicago by Jack Webster to Cleveland, where Ernie Allison was waiting to fly it over the "hell stretch" route across the Alleghenies. At Hazelhurst Field, Long

Island, Allison turned over six mail pouches to Division Superintendent J.E. Whitbeck. The entire flight from the moment that Farr Nutter had pushed the throttle forward at Crissy Field outside San Francisco until Ernie Allison switched off his engine at Hazelhurst had taken 33 hours and 25 minutes. Actual flying time was 25 hours, 53 minutes for an average ground speed of just over 103 miles per hour.

Assistant Postmaster General Otto Praeger, the one postal official above all others who believed in the airmail, promptly issued a statement:

> The all-night flight from Cheyenne, Wyoming, to Chicago, a distance of 839 miles, of San Francisco mail bound for New York by the regular equipment of the Airmail Service, is the most momentous step in civil aviation. The Postmaster General some time ago directed that the airmail enter upon regular night operations, and the flight by a pilot never over the ground before, in black night, through snow flurries and fog drifts, with three landings for refueling and exchange of mail, is a demonstration of the entire

James H. "Jack" Knight (in cockpit), "the ace of the Air Mail Service," whose daring flight in hazardous weather made newspaper headlines in February, 1921. Knight made the 839-mile flight from Cheyenne, Wyoming, to Chicago at night through snow and fog with three landings for fuel and exchange of mail.

feasibility of commercial night flying. It will mean the speedy revolutionizing of the letter transportation methods and practices throughout the world.

The Postmaster General had indeed "directed that the airmail enter upon regular night operations" and had issued orders on August 20, 1920, to install radio stations along the transcontinental route. This network of ground stations was put into operation during 1921 and 1922 and was used to relay weather reports and routine messages between stations. In the meantime, a young Army Air Service officer, Lieutenant Donald L. Bruner, stationed at McCook Field near Dayton, began experimenting with lighting equipment that would assure safe landings and take-offs at night. He eventually designed the type of airplane landing light basically in use today after trying ordinary automobile headlamps, motion picture projector bulbs, and wingtip searchlights.

During 1921, working with Lieutenant Harold R. Harris, Bruner established the first lighted airway between McCook Field and Columbus, Ohio, 80 miles away. He developed rotating beacons, field floodlights, and flashing identifying lights which enabled pilots to fly from one beacon to another, to know exactly where they were along the airway, and to land at their destinations safely. Bruner was eventually awarded the Distinguished Flying Cross for developing and perfecting night flying equipment, thus making it possible for military and commercial airplanes to traverse the length and breadth of the United States during the hours of darkness.

In spite of Jack Knight's heroic effort at night mail flying in February, 1921, no further steps were taken to fly the mail after dark until the next year when Colonel Paul Henderson was appointed chief of the Airmail Service. He was not a pilot, but, like Ben Lipsner, he was a visionary who could see beyond the horizon in the field of aviation. He believed that 24-hour airmail service could be made practical, when it was felt that the service should be turned over to civilian operations under contract so that the Government could get out of the day-to-day operations.

Henderson watched the development of the Army's lighted airway experiment with great interest. In 1923 he directed the establishment of the first lighted segment of the Wilson Airway between Chicago and Cheyenne. Lighted emergency landing fields equipped with rotating gas beacons were constructed every 25 to 30 miles along this route. Newly modified DH-4's with landing lights were added to the Post Office fleet. An Airmail Repair Depot was established at Chicago, and pilots were given extensive training in night landings and airways navigation. When these arrangements were complete, a four-day test period was begun, whereby the mail was flown cross-country both ways on a regular schedule. The run between Chicago and Cheyenne was made at night.

The experiment proceeded without a hitch. Mail was flown both ways across the continent without a single accident. The best time eastbound during the four-day trial period was 26 hours, 14 minutes; westbound, 29 hours, 38 minutes. The reason for the lower eastbound time was due to the prevailing westerly winds that increase the speed of planes going from west to east.

The remainder of 1923 and the first half of 1924 were spent in preparing for the inauguration of a regular transcontinental service which was to begin on July 1, 1924. In the interim, the lighted airway was extended until it reached from New York to Salt Lake City. Flying of the mail at night soon became routine. As a tribute to those responsible, the Airmail Service was awarded the famous Collier Trophy in 1923 and 1924 "for the greatest achievement in aviation in America."

Just as Ben Lipsner, Otto Praeger, Paul Henderson, and a few others had predicted, the establishment of day-night operations caused a tremendous upsurge of airmail usage. The DeHavillands were rapidly wearing out. Newer and larger planes had to be procured. The Post Office Department asked for a competition within the newly established aircraft industry and, as a result, the Douglas Aircraft Company won a sale of 51 specially-designed mail planes that would carry twice the load of the DH-4's for greater non-stop distances and at much higher speeds. These were placed on the routes and quickly established new speed records. The fastest trip on any route was made on the Chicago – Cleveland run on January 30, 1927, when an average speed of 175.1 miles per hour was attained.

Since it had never been the intention of the Government to operate airmail planes permanently, legislation was asked for and passed in 1925 to enable the Post Office Department to contract with private firms for carrying the mail. Called the Kelly Act, it was the nation's first airmail law and had as its purpose "to encourage commercial aviation and to authorize the Postmaster General to contract for airmail service." It was this act of Congress which fathered the airlines and provided aviation interests with the incentive to form operating companies. It also encouraged private capital to invest in them.

Chapter 4

The Airmail Service was phased out over a year's period, and on July 30, 1927, the last mails were carried by pilots under the direction of the Post Office Department. The record had been both good and bad. The original 218-mile route between New York and Washington had been extended coast to coast over 2,680 route miles. During the last year of operation, pilots had flown 17,500,000 letters over 2,500,000 miles. About 40 percent of this mileage had been flown in darkness, and the overall rate of schedules met was 94 percent.

The nine years of operation had cost Uncle Sam $15,000,000. Thirty-two pilots and nine mechanics had been killed in line of duty. Three hundred planes had crashed; however, most of them had been salvaged and at least some of the parts had flown again.

Again, another chapter in the history of the airmail closed. Brave airmen had served their country in the name of progress. Some of them had died; others had been crippled and scarred for life. But the survivors had learned from the mistakes and bad luck of the others and, in the process, had pushed back the barriers to aeronautical progress.

5

TALES OF THE AIRMAIL SERVICE

ONE OF THE FIRST WRITERS to describe the hazards of flying the transcontinental route coast to coast was John Goldstrom, a freelance writer. He had arranged with the Scripps-Howard newspaper syndicate to do a series of articles on the airmail and had received the reluctant permission of Postmaster General Albert S. Burleson to fly from New York to San Francisco with a sack of mail. To "make it legal," Goldstrom had been appointed a special agent of the Airmail Service to make a public report on the operation as he witnessed it. On the morning of December 28, 1920, he shoe-horned himself into the front cockpit of a DH-4 at Hazelhurst Field, Long Island. His pilot on the route to Cleveland was Wesley L. Smith, just out of the hospital after healing from burns suffered in a recent crash. Goldstrom described the first leg of the flight:

The air was frosty and bit sharply through my flying clothes as we headed west against a 25-mile wind and crossed over New York; then over the icy Hudson and through snow over the Jersey Palisades. Over the Alleghenies in Pennsylvania the ship plunged and pitched violently against gusty winds. We ran into fog and more snow. The mail pit had not been constructed for passenger comfort, and as I was sitting a bit too high, on mail sacks and behind a makeshift windshield, I caught the icy gale of the propeller wash. I became severely airsick, thought of excellent excuses for abandoning the flight at the first stop, and then became utterly indifferent to the evident possibility that the stop might be made in a tree in the upper Alleghenies. For a low ceiling was forcing Smith to skim the wooded mountains so closely that it was found afterward that our landing gear had snatched a branch from one of the trees—lurching through the clouds at nearly a mile and a half a minute.

At Bellefonte, Pa., the half-way stop for fuel, tender hands pried me loose from the mail pit. I was almost literally frozen stiff. We had been in the air a little less than three hours. Field Manager M. J. Kelly advised me to call the flight off for the day, but I managed to climb back into the cockpit for the remainder of the run to Cleveland. Cramps and chills enlivened this part of the flight. It was about ten below zero at three thousand feet. We landed at Martin Field, just east of Cleveland, about three o'clock, having flown from New York in a bit less than five and a half hours of flying time.

At the Cleveland station the kindly John Whitbeck, division superintendent there, slapped and massaged warmth into my frozen flesh. Pilot Smith's black mustache had been frapped to Arctic whiteness by frost. He was appropriately complimented by another pilot on having kept a stiff upper lip through one of the roughest airmail runs since the division was organized.

Goldstrom pressed on westward with pilots W. D. Williams, Walter J. Smith, and Harry H. Rowe. At Omaha the plucky writer bragged about his good luck and the speed he was making as an airmail passenger. Bill Votaw, superintendent at the midpoint station, remarked, "You have ahead of you the windy plains of Nebraska, the buttes of Wyoming, the Rockies, and the Sierras. You'll be real lucky if you don't run into a little grief before you get to 'Frisco.'"

Votaw was not kidding, as Goldstrom quickly discovered. In the next few days he experienced five forced landings. He described the last of his escapes from injury or death:

The Salt Lake airfield of those days was one of the worst on the route, and it was necessary to hurdle steeply over telephone wires at one end of the short runway. This maneuver loosened several of my back teeth. It was preliminary to hurdling the awesome Ruby Range at 13,400 feet, with less than a hundred feet of clearance and some of the roughest flying I have ever experienced. But two and a half hours after leaving the Utah capital, we landed at Elko, Nevada.

Field Manager Barbour sent us off toward Reno in a stiffening wind. As we neared the edge of the Alkali Flats things began to happen. A seventy-mile hurricane rushed at us from behind Granite Peak, and in the next few minutes seemed undecided as to whether to dash us against a mountain or throw us to the desert floor. It compromised by blowing us into a terrific dust storm, which we were told afterward was the worst the Nevada desert country had seen in years.

The storm had forced Mouton far off course when an overheated engine compelled him to find a landing place. How he got us down without spattering us over the Nevada landscape I never have comprehended. We landed on the desert, after bounding over or crashing through half a dozen clumps of sagebrush, with a broken right wing.

It was just past high noon when we came down, but it couldn't be proved by the sun, which was invisible in an atmosphere full of swirling dust. We crouched for four hours in our cockpits, waiting for the storm to die down. We were unable to see ten feet in any direction. It was nearly five o'clock when the sun became faintly visible not far above the western horizon. In the dusty haze it appeared as a light green disc, the work of an impressionist scene painter.

We discussed whether it would be best to wait for a rescue party or start on foot in the general direction of a ranch which Mouton had seen from the air. Shortly after five o'clock, with darkness coming on, we decided to start out armed only with a broken wing skid against night-prowling mountain lions or wild cats.

There are more pleasant forms of exercise than walking over the mushy "self-rising" ground of the Nevada desert country, especially when the stroller is dressed in heavy fur-lined flying clothes. I was to learn that a lot of shoe-leather can be worn out in cross-country flying.

Darkness descended quickly and a light snow began to fall. The sky was cloudy, but there were a few stars to steer by; and Mouton was aided in his orientation of our course by two mountain ranges. We learned later that we were in the Buena Vista Valley.

We trudged through the desert all night, walking until it became necessary to rest, and resuming when it became too cold to rest any longer. . . . That sunrise was the most beautiful I have ever seen anywhere in the world.

During the night we had begun to fear that we were not on the right course. We were without water or food, and stories of men lost in the desert under such circumstances, and what happened to them, came easily to mind. The occasional sight of a whitened skull—although those we saw were of animals—didn't help any.

But the clear winter morning was not far advanced when we saw a ranch in the distance. Mouton's calculations had been about perfect. We trudged on, and reached the Hudgins ranch house before noon.

D. E. Hudgins told us later that we had walked about twenty-five miles. An eastbound mail pilot had last seen us as we passed Battle Mountain in the storm, and when we did not arrive at Reno it was thought unlikely that we could have lived through a forced landing under the circumstances. Newspapers reported us a probable casualties of airmail pioneering.

Hudgins said we had been lucky to escape attack in the desert by crazed coyotes. A coyote in its right mind will not attack a man, but Hudgins told us that a ranger had conceived the brilliant notion of inoculating several captured coyotes with rabies germs and turning them loose in the desert, figuring that they would spread hydrophobia and kill one another off. Instead the crazed animals had come boldly into the ranches, attacking human beings and animals indiscriminately. Four men had lost their lives.

We saw one coyote, but evidently it was not infected, for it scampered off when we approached.

From the ranch Mouton telephoned the Reno airmail station, reported that we were safe, and learned that planes had been sent out to search for us. Pilot Farr Nutter, when his fuel was nearly exhausted, had seen on the desert something that appeared to be a burned and wrecked plane. He had flown on to Lovelock, the nearest town, for more fuel, intending to return and investigate further. He was reached by telephone and informed that we were safe.

Thirteen days after he had left New York, Goldstrom landed at the Presidio in San Francisco. He had a healthy respect for the pilots who risked their necks on a daily basis to prove that mail could be moved from coast to coast on a regular schedule. He summed up his respect by saying:

"I have sat at many an aeronautical banquet and heard high praise heaped upon the heads of this or that politically appointed official under whose administration the Airmail advanced and became successful, but I have joined in the applause only when the speaker got around to mentioning the pilots."*

After each flight the Airmail Service pilots would turn in brief reports concerning the condition of their planes, the weather encountered, or anything unusual they may have observed on the ground that could help the next pilot to fly over the route. However, when an accident, forced landing, or untoward incident occurred, they were required to submit a little more information for the record. Here is one such report by Paul P. Scott, who flew the westbound night mail out of Salt Lake City in December, 1924:

I encountered snow and mist, and visibility was very poor as far as Silver Zone Pass. The weather cleared at Shafter excepting ground fog banks to the north, west and south. I headed south to go around the mountain range when I noticed a small hole between the fog bank and the clouds through Saddle Pass on the regular course. The low-

Post Office Department "aerial mail" pilots were authorized to wear these wings. Extremely scarce, they are worth hundreds of dollars today. The wings of present Northwest Airlines pilots today contain the words "U.S. Air Mail."

*Goldstrom, John, "The Uncovered Wagon," *Popular Aviation*, May, 1929.

est part of the Saddle is about 300 feet wide and can be cleared at 7,200 feet. On each side of the Saddle the altitude of the range is about 8,500 feet.

No part of the mountain range was visible. I had proceeded through the hole, my altimeter registering 7,800 feet, to what I thought to be half-way through, when the hole closed up in front. I banked the plane and was turning to come out when the fog closed in behind me and visibility was then not over 20 feet. No sooner had I leveled off the plane and started climbing than I saw I was scraping the tops off cedar trees.

I pulled the throttle and the stick back together and crashed on the slope of the Saddle about 8,200 feet.

When I came to, my face was buried in the snow and I was groping for the switches with my right hand, my left arm and hand feeling numb and useless. But I could not locate them, so I unfastened my belt and dug enough snow to pull myself from under, a convenient cedar limb being handy.

The plane was completely washed out. My left shoulder was out of place and my left arm freezing rapidly. I noticed I had cigarettes and matches but that I had left my gun in Salt Lake. There was a heavy fog with no sun visible by which to get my bearings; and I also considered I was extremely lucky to be able to notice anything at all.

I started down the mountain side to what I thought to be the general direction of the road through the Saddle. The snow was deep and the mountain steep which made walking difficult.

I slipped on some shale rock, striking my left shoulder, and knocked it back into place. I rubbed my left arm and hand with snow until it thawed out and felt normal. I walked down to the road. The visibility was better at low altitude. I walked to the railroad tracks and flagged a passenger train. I then sent a wire from Wells, Nevada, the first stop.

Sudden, unpredicted storms were still a serious threat to pilots, even though lighted emergency fields and 500-million-candlepower floodlights had been installed along the airmail routes. Frank Yager, flying the eastbound mail from Cheyenne to Omaha, left Cheyenne at 8:30 P.M., ahead of an approaching storm. It lay far to the north parallel to his course, and he figured he could make it to Omaha. One hundred and twenty miles out of Cheyenne, just as he was passing over Lodgepole, Nebraska, the broken clouds above him suddenly closed and shut out the stars. He knew immediately that he had encountered a strong cross wind from his left. He arrived over the Chappell search-light and was about to continue toward the flashing beacon at Big Spring when, even as he looked, the beacon suddenly disap-peared. A huge black curtain had been drawn across the horizon in the form of an angry frontal thunderstorm. His plane began to buck and pitch violently.

There was only one course of action to be taken as far as Yager was concerned. He banked steeply, cut his throttle, and started a glide for the Chappell emergency field, intending to land into the wind toward the east. He hoped to get his ship on the ground and tied down before the storm hit. As he was approaching the field boundary, a vicious downdraft slammed the DH-4 into the ground before he could cross the fence. His terse report explained what happened:

> Found myself sitting on the prairie clear of the ship, with a terrific wind blowing from the west, exactly opposite to its direction the minute before. All I could see of the wreck was the lighted cockpit turned toward me.
>
> Didn't feel any effects of being hurt, so groped for my flashlight in the cockpit, turned out the lights, and stum-bled down the hill to the beacon tower.
>
> I regret to report that the plane is one of the most thor-oughly wrecked aircraft I ever saw.

One of the biggest problems during the early days of the air-mail was to find caretakers and ground personnel at the route stations who could understand the needs of the pilots. The green farm lads hired generally knew next to nothing about mechanical things connected with aviation, and this ignorance meant that pilots had to be able to repair the ground radios and light beacons along the route, as well as repair their own planes and service them. The burden was so great that one pilot, Marion S. "Dog" Collins, remarked that airmail pilots had so much to remember they were all stoop-shouldered.

One pilot on a westbound run was worried about the weather at his next stop. He called ahead on the telephone and asked, "How high is your ceiling there?"

There was a pause and a young voice answered, "About ten feet, I think. If you'll wait a minute I'll measure it!"

Crashes of airmail planes were frequent, resulting in injuries and death. Most were the result of flying into bad weather without proper instruments and navigation aids.

Another pilot put a call through to a caretaker at one of the Nebraska fields and asked, "How's your weather out there?"

The answer was quick but uninformative, "Not so bad for this time of year. How's yours?"

Once the field caretakers had a fair understanding of what a pilot needed to know about the weather, information was a little more meaningful, but pilots still had their troubles. This conversation between pilot and caretaker took place on the telephone in 1923:

Pilot: "Hello, Caretaker, this is the pilot of the eastbound run to Chicago. What's your visibility there?"

Caretaker: "What's my what?"

Pilot: "What's your visibility? How far can you see?"

Caretaker: "Ain't seein' so good this morning. Broke my glasses."

Pilot:	"Sorry to hear that. What's the weather like?"
Caretaker:	"Don't think it's so good."
Pilot:	"Well, what's it like?"
Caretaker:	"Storm's comin'. Can feel it. My corns ache like fierce."
Pilot:	"That's too bad. But what kind of weather do you have right now?"
Caretaker:	"Fair to middlin'."
Pilot:	"Can you see across the field?"
Caretaker:	"Told you. Broke my glasses."
Pilot:	"Anybody else there?"
Caretaker:	"Just my boy. He's fifteen. Real smart."
Pilot:	"Put him on."
Boy:	"Yessir?"
Pilot:	"Son, look out the window of the shack and tell me how far you can see."
Boy:	" 'Bout thirty feet."
Pilot:	"Fog?"
Boy:	"No. Hay wagon parked outside the shack. Can't see over it."
Pilot:	(after cursing lightly to himself) "Son, do me a favor. Go outside and look up at the sky, at the clouds. See if the sun is out. Look across the field and tell me how far you can see, what object you can see that is the farthest away from you that you recognize."
Boy:	(after long silence) "Mister, I done like you said. Sun's out. Clouds is real purty a'rushin' past. Saw my new calf a followin' its mother in the next pasture."
Pilot:	"How far's that?"
Boy:	"Can't say."
Pilot:	"Why not?"

Boy: "Cow and calf is runnin' too fast."

Pilot: "Why are they running?"

Boy: "Bad storm's comin'."

Pilot: "Oh?"

Boy: "Mister, I'm goin' to have to hang up now. Pa's yellin' at me to come help him get the cows in the barn. Wind just blew the hay wagon over and our windmill's about to go. Call us back when the storm's over!"

The airmail pilot who never became lost on his route at one time or another was a rarity. One pilot, flying the route from Chicago to Cleveland, deviated far to the south of his course to get around a thunderstorm. After two hours he was hopelessly lost and decided to land in a pasture where he saw a farmer working. He landed and taxied up to the surprised man and yelled, "Where's Cleveland?"

The farmer stared at the pilot a moment and then yelled back, "Haven't you heard? Cleveland's dead!"

Forced landings in rough country were frequently disastrous, if not for the pilot, certainly for the plane. Sometimes, however, both plane and pilot would survive to fly another day. On the "main line" between Salt Lake City and Cheyenne one day, Frank Crisson found himself flying under a lowering ceiling. He was following the highway below into Cheyenne and gradually went lower and lower. He ran into a snow squall and couldn't see ahead more than a few hundred feet. He decided to execute the 180° turn maneuver, known by the airmail pilots as "getting the hell out," and began his turn, hoping he wouldn't hit the walls of rock he knew were on both sides of the road.

Suddenly, Crisson heard—nothing. There was absolutely dead silence. Shaking his head in disbelief, he thought at first he was dead. Then he realized that he had crashed into a snowbank in full flight and had come to a sudden but safe stop.

Crisson looked at his watch and remembered that he was to make a position report. The radio worked so he called Cheyenne Radio and reported his position as "63$\frac{1}{2}$ miles west of Cheyenne."

The Cheyenne operation was quiet a moment, then asked Crisson how he knew he was exactly 63$\frac{1}{2}$ miles out.

"Because I'm sitting beside a highway sign that says 'Cheyenne—63¹/₂ miles,' that's how!"

Parachutes were not used by airmail pilots until late 1922. Many pilots could never have used one successfully because they would never fly high enough, while others were not only glad to wear them but used them to save their necks when their flying luck ran out. This story is about the most famous airmail pilot in history.

The Transcontinental Airmail route had been in operation for some time when the St. Louis–Chicago route began. At first there were no light beacons and no emergency fields between the two cities, and the planes used on the route had no radios or landing lights. A pilot was on his own and had to depend entirely upon his own judgment, skill, and luck. He took off whenever he thought there was a chance to get through, and flew as far as possible. When the weather got bad, he landed wherever he could and sent the mail on by train.

One of the first men to be hired on this new route was a tall, thin man with a boyish face. He had a shy smile and a dreamy, faraway look in his dark blue eyes. The other pilots called him "Slim."

Slim had been chosen to make the first night flight out of Chicago and had been flying the route for several months. One night in September, 1926, after take-off from St. Louis, ground fog formed underneath him as he droned along. The white sheet covering the dark earth gradually grew thicker and reached upward for 600 feet. Slim kept well above it and flew a compass course toward Chicago, hoping he would soon find an opening. As he neared the time when the Windy City should be beneath him, all he could see was a dull glow through the misty whiteness caused by the city lights below.

It was a frustrating feeling to be flying around over his destination and not being able to pierce the ground cloud that blotted the airport from his view. After churning around the city for 30 minutes, Slim was convinced that no holes were going to open up. He headed west, thinking he might spot one of the light beacons on the transcontinental route. This was unsuccessful so he headed southwest, hoping to strike the edge of fog south of the Illinois River. After another half-hour of flying, his engine suddenly stopped. He quickly switched to the emergency gas tank. Only 20 minutes of fuel remained.

There was now only one thing Slim could do besides bail out. He let down on top of the thick white blanket until his wheels were skimming the wispy tops and released a flare. The flare burned brightly but quickly sank out of sight into the misty whiteness. Now he had no choice.

Slim pushed the throttle forward and climbed up into the night until his altimeter read 5,000 feet. The engine sputtered and died. Without hesitation, he unbuckled his safety belt, eased his tall frame out of the cockpit, and went over the side. Later, in his official report of the incident, Slim wrote:

> "I was falling head downward when the risers jerked me into an upright position and the 'chute opened . . . I pulled the flashlight from my belt and was playing it down toward the top of the fog when I heard the plane's engine pick up. . . ."

Slim had forgotten to cut the switches in his craft before bailing out. Without his weight the plane nosed down, allowing some of the gasoline in the bottom of the tank to enter the carburetor. The engine caught and the windmilling propeller made it run wide open. Slim could hear the plane circling as he drifted through the white nothingness that surrounded him. Five times the roaring noise went around him in the mist; it seemed to come dangerously close. Suddenly the noise stopped, and Slim knew that the plane had finally run out of gas. Before he was ready for it, he slammed into the ground and tumbled end over end as his 'chute dragged him along a row of cornstalks. Unbuckling the straps, he shed the harness and checked himself over. No broken bones, not even a scratch!

Slim made his way to a farm house and asked for help to locate his crashed plane. A farmer finally found it about a mile away. Slim reported:

> The plane was wound up in a ball-shaped mess. It had narrowly missed one farm house and had hooked the left wing in a grain shock a quarter mile beyond. The ship had landed on the left wing and wheel and skidded along the ground for 80 yards, going through one fence before coming to rest in the edge of a cornfield about 100 yards short of a barn. The mail pit was laid open and one sack of mail was on the ground. The mail, however, was uninjured.
>
> The sheriff at Ottawa arrived, and we took the mail to the Ottawa post office to be entrained at 3:30 A.M. for Chicago.

Crashes of airmail planes were frequent, resulting in injuries and death. Most were the result of flying into bad weather without proper instruments and navigation aids.

Chapter 5

This successful jump was actually the third Slim had made. He had first used a parachute in March, 1925, when he was involved in a mid-air collision as a pilot in the Army Air Service Reserve. He had jumped a second time three months later when his plane wouldn't pull out of a spin.

Just seven weeks after the third jump described here, Slim was again on the Chicago – St. Louis run when he ran into a blinding snowstorm. This time, however, he remembered to shut off the switches and left the plane at 10,000 feet. Again he landed safely, rescued the mail, and sent it on its way by train.

In just two years, this young pilot had saved his life four times by using the parachute. In all aviation history to this day, only one other pilot has equalled this record.* But this is not what has caused Slim's name to go down in aviation history. Five months after his fourth jump, he became the first man to fly across the Atlantic Ocean nonstop and alone. Slim's full name was Charles Augustus Lindbergh.

As the transcontinental airmail route proved successful, the Post Office Department authorized new routes and hired pilots to fly them. It was decided that service should be inaugurated in Alaska, provided a reliable pilot could be found. That pilot was Carl Ben Eielson, a former schoolteacher who had decided that the lure of the cockpit was greater than that of the classroom.

Eielson made his first mail flight on February 21, 1924, when he inaugurated the route between Fairbanks and McGrath. The 260-mile trail he blazed in the air proved that the flying machine could replace the dogsled and that regular and frequent delivery of mail by air was possible in the Arctic.

Following is the report Eielson made to his superiors in the Post Office Department:

> Our landing field, which is 1,200 feet long and 600 feet wide and surrounded by low scrubby trees, was covered with from two to three feet of snow. The snow up here is of a very light, dry, powdery variety. It does not pack well, as is the case in the States, because there is so little moisture in it. The skis on the airplane dug about a foot and a half into the snow, thus making it impossible to taxi except by using about 1,300 rpm. I find that the wide skis are more practical for this country.
>
> The thermometer registered five below zero at the start of the first trip. There was no wind. The sky was about two-

---

*Pilot Officer Tony Woods-Scawen, RAF.

thirds overcast with clouds, which lay at an elevation of 4,500 feet.

I carried 164 pounds of mail, a full set of tools, a mountain sheep sleeping bag, ten days' provisions, five gallons oil, snowshoes, a gun, an ax, and spare parts. My clothing consisted of two pairs of heavy woolen hose, a pair of caribou socks, a pair of moccasins reaching over the knees, one suit heavy underwear, a pair of khaki breeches, a pair of heavy trousers of Hudson Bay duffle over that, a heavy shirt, a sweater, a marten skin cap, goggles, and over that a loose reindeer skin parka, which had a hood on it with wolverine skin around it.

Wolverine skin is fine around the face because it does not frost. On my hands I wore a pair of light woolen gloves and a heavy fur mitt over that. I found I had too much clothing on even when I had the exhaust heater turned off. At five below zero I was too warm. I could fly in 40-below weather in perfect comfort with this outfit and the engine heater. On my second trip I cut out the caribou socks, the duffle trousers, and the heavy fur mittens and was entirely comfortable.

May I not suggest to the Department that all mail pilots be supplied with reindeer skin parkas and large size moccasins. I have worn the fur jumpers that are in use outside and it is my opinion that they are not to be compared with the parkas. This is the consensus of opinion among the old-timers here, who have tried everything to ward off the cold. The parkas are knee length, they are very light, they pull over the neck so no wind can blow in through the flaps.

The following are the advantages of the parkas:

1. Cost only $40 for a good one.
2. Light and roomy. Do not bind.
3. Have a hood on them which can be pulled over the head and tied so that only the eyes are exposed. The fur around the hood is wolverine so it does not frost.
4. Can jump in and out of planes as well with one on as if you did not have it on.
5. In case of forced landing, pilot could walk as well with it on as off. It is impossible to wear the jumper as it is too heavy for walking.
6. Greatest warmth for its weight.

The moccasins are advantageous because they are light, warm, and comfortable. As many pairs of stockings as are necessary can be put on. The rudder can be felt all the time, thus giving better control.

I took off the field on February 21 at 8:45 A.M. The skis dug into the snow until I got up a little speed then gradually lifted out. I ran 800 feet before I felt the snow. I turned the motor to 1,450 rpm until off the ground. I then cut it to 1,300. I turned the motor from 1,250 to 1,350 on the trip. The motor never missed coming or going. The tachometer did not work steadily, but the engine was perfect. My airspeed indicator did not work at all and my compass was off about 40 degrees in some direction on account of magnetism in the engine. Both of these I have since corrected. As I am well acquainted with the country over which I am flying I did not depend on my compass except to follow relative readings taken by pointing the plane at landmarks which I knew.

After testing the motor and balance, I hit my course. The first 50 miles I followed the Tanana River, which is a fair emergency field though the ice is a little rough in places. At Nenana, a town of about 100 inhabitants, I left the Tanana and steered across the country. I veered to the left of a straight course in order to follow the flat country and stay near the roadhouses, which are located on the mail trail at intervals of about 35 miles.

After about an hour and a half I spotted Lake Minchumina to my right. I was then halfway between the lake and Mt. McKinley, each of them probably 30 miles away. I passed to the left of the Munsatli Mountains and a little later saw the main Kuskokwim River, which I followed in to McGrath, my destination. I landed on the Tacotna River at McGrath at 11:35. It took me 2 hours and 50 minutes to cover 260 miles, straight course, and I had a slight favorable breeze. The way I had come I had covered about 315 miles. There was about a foot of snow on the river; an excellent landing field. I came down smoothly, sliding about 500 feet after the skis first touched the snow. As I had plenty of room, I intentionally made a fast landing.

The mail was transferred to dog team, the gas tank was filled with the same kind of gasoline (Domestic Aviation Gasoline—about 62 B test), three gallons of Mobil B were added to what was left in the tank. (I cannot change oil over there as there is no Mobile B there.) The thrust bearing was filled with oil, clearances checked, and engine inspected.

Then had lunch, loaded on 60 pounds of mail (which was all they had), and started the motor. I had no experienced help whatsoever as no one over there had ever seen a plane. It was difficult to start the Liberty all alone. I got a man to hold my hand while I swung the propeller, no one being in the cockpit. It will be easier from now on as I am instructing a helper at McGrath.

I left McGrath at 2:35 P.M.—that was the earliest I could get ready on first trip. I knew this was pretty late as darkness descends early here in February. I did not want to stay over as the day was good and I thought it might be very difficult to start the motor after it stood out all night in the cold and it would be hard on the motor. As there was no wind I thought I could get back in better time by flying a little faster and taking a straighter course. I expected to get home by 5:10 P.M.—that is, just at dusk.

I flew over Appel Mountain and one hour and fifteen minutes later I reached Lake Minchumina, which is nearly the halfway point. This was on schedule so I thought I was all right. Later I passed over a stream which was not on my map and I thought it must be the Kantishna River. Later I reached the Kantishna River and I thought it was the Tanana River as it was time for me to be nearing Nenana. To the left I saw a bluff that looked like the Nenana bluff; I checked it further by noticing a river going around the bluff, but I was positive that it was Nenana when I saw a river entering the Tanana at the point where the Nenana River enters the Tanana at the town of Nenana.

I struck for the bluff, and everything was all right excepting that the town of Nenana was not in its place. I knew I must have veered to the left so I started up the Tanana to find Nenana. I followed it for half an hour, that is, 50 miles.

By this time it was pitch-dark. I could not believe that I had got 50 miles off my course after the same compass course had brought me to Lake Minchumina halfway, and this was exactly on the course. I could not see the lights of Nenana so I left the river, going east. I thought I must have got on the Kantishna River and that I was following it back to Mt. McKinley as the country looked flat in the pitch-darkness. The sky was entirely overcast—not a star showed.

I wandered about completely lost for most of an hour, then I knew that the river I had left was the Tanana. About this time I saw a light, so I cut my altitude and went down to it. It must have been a trapper's cabin near the Chatanika River. I was tempted to set the ship down there and have a nice place to sleep, but I knew I would wreck the ship if I did, so I decided to look around some more. I went back to the big river I had left, and when I was following it down I saw a flare in the distance. I hit for it and it turned out to be my home field. There was a light in front of the hangar. I guessed at the extremity of the field and went in. I hit a tree in gliding and broke off one ski. In landing, I nosed over and broke my propeller. The trouble was all fixed up in three days and the plane ready to go again.

The entire town had been waiting at the field for more than an hour. I had been in the air four hours and ten minutes on the return trip. I landed at 6:45 P.M. I had been in the air seven hours that day, covering a distance farther than from Fairbanks to Siberia, Fairbanks to Point Barrow, or Fairbanks to Juneau. This seems incredible in Alaska for it takes a month of hardship at this time of the year to go from here to Nome by the fastest route—dog team.

Other reports received by the Department were not so matter-of-fact or detailed. Dean C. Smith, a mail pilot who later went on an expedition to the South Pole with Admiral Richard E. Byrd, had to write up the results of a forced landing. Not a man to waste words, his report is a classic: "Dead-sticked—flying low—only place available—on cow—killed cow—wrecked plane—scared me. Smith."

Another pilot, Kenneth Unger, had similar bad luck with a forced landing. He reported:

I was crossing the Rubbie Mountains at 10,500 feet when I broke a set of gears and landed in a very small field in the Secret Pass. A rancher riding range saw me land and rode over and let me take his horse to ride to the nearest ranch.

After phoning to Elko for help, I started back to the ship on horse. I started to mount and the horse took off in a climbing turn before I got in the seat and had my safety belt fastened.

To make a long story short, I over-controlled her nose, went down and I spun—or side-slipped, I don't know which—into the ground at great speed.

I broke my left ankle and was well shaken up in my second landing.

After filling the air with smoke for a few minutes, I got the beast again and we took off in a gentle loop and returned to the ship. Help came. We repaired the motor and I flew the ship to Elko. There I had the ankle set by the best doctor in town.

I had to borrow a pair of crutches made for a man six foot tall and as I am five foot seven we got along fine. I had the boys at the field tack a strip to the right rudder bar so I could pull as well as push. This made up for the loss of my left foot. I took off for Salt Lake with the regular mail as usual.

Motto: Always be sure you have your safety belt on before you take off with a western horse.

Looking back on those early days, it is difficult to imagine that the early airmail pilots flew without adequate maps. Those they did have were without elevations or any symbols of value to a pilot. They were road maps which were intended for the early motorist who only wanted to know how to get from one town to another by the best road. Pilots never saw contour maps and never knew for certain how high the mountains were that they crossed. Most pilots kept pocket notebooks in which they noted

Five airmail pilots pose in their winter flying gear.

the height of silos, train schedules, distances, and the names of farmers along their routes who had telephones.

Recognizing the need for route information, the Post Office Department first published a *Book of Directions* in 1921. Following is a sample of the route information for a pilot leaving Hazelhurst Field, Long Island, for Bellefonte, Pennsylvania:

> Follow the tracks of the Long Island Railroad past Belmont Park Race Track, keeping Jamaica on the left. Cross New York City over the lower end of Central Park.
>
> Twenty-five miles to Newark, N.J., Heller Field is located in Newark and may be identified as follows: The field is 1¼ miles west of the Passaic River and lies in the V formed by the Green Lake Division and Orange branch of the New York, Lake Erie and Western Railroad. The Morris Canal bounds the western edge of the field. The roof of the large steel hangar is painted an orange color.
>
> Thirty miles to Orange Mountains. Cross the Orange Mountains over a small round lake or pond. Slightly to the right will be seen the polo field and golf course of Essex Country Club. About 8 miles to the north is Mountain Lake, easily seen after crossing the Orange Mountains. . . .

Training of airmail pilots was just as "primitive" as the instructions they carried. The best method was for a new pilot to follow another on the route he would fly. Veteran pilot Ernest M. Allison was assigned to teach Charles H. Ames "the ropes" shortly after the latter joined the Airmail Service. Ames described his initial flight as he followed Allison over the route from Bellefonte to Cleveland:

> I encountered fog and low ceiling at Brookville, Pa., making it impossible to use a map. I know my only chance was to follow Allie. Soon I noticed we were flying down a small river which led us into a larger one. We were about a hundred feet apart and about twenty-five feet above the water, zooming the bridges with the ceiling below the banks of the river when we ran into a smoke bank caused by a freight train which filled the river with smoke.
>
> I slowed down, thought of my past sins and my favorite flowers. We were flying blind and I didn't want to hit Allie, or the ground, going any faster than I could help.
>
> When I came out of the smoke, I happened to catch a glimpse of Allie making a left turn some distance ahead.

Map of early airmail routes flown by civilian pilots after the routes were completely turned over to civilian contractors in 1927.

U. S. Airways as of December 31, 1927.

LEGEND

═══ Lighted portions Dec. 31, 1927
─── Non-lighted portions Dec. 31, 1927
═══ Non-mail routes, unlighted

When I came to a creek I also turned to the left, but found no Allie in sight. I was lost in terrible country and flying a Curtiss HA which I couldn't land in less than one hundred acres!

Soon I came to a fork in the creek and, remembering that Allie turned to the left before, I turned up the left branch (a 50-50 chance since I had no compass) and came upon a lake seemingly in the mountains with the ceiling still below the banks. About three hundred feet ahead and about twenty-five feet off the water I saw Allie.

What a grand and glorious feeling!

Upon our arrival at Cleveland, I found that Allie had taken me down the Clarion River to the Allegheny River, up the Allegheny to Sandy Creek; up Sandy Creek and past Sandy Lake to Greenville, north from Greenville into a valley to Lake Erie and down the lake to Cleveland. Several times since, this experience has made it possible for me to get through in bad weather.

Ames' luck did not remain so good. On the night of October 1, 1925, he left Hadley Field near New Brunswick, New Jersey, for Bellefonte. He never reached his destination. In a dense fog, he ran out of luck and altitude at the same time eight miles east of Bellefonte.

The airmail pilots, daredevils though they were, knew that any flight might be their last—that their luck might run out at any moment. One of those who had a premonition that he might not return from a mail flight was Captain Leonard Brooke Hyde-Pearson who was assigned to the New York – Cleveland route. He wrote a letter, sealed it, and inscribed on the envelope, "To Be Opened Only After My Death." He placed it away with his personal belongings in his apartment.

Pearson also met his fate near Bellefonte, in a thickening fog. He crashed into the side of a mountain while trying to find his way out of a box canyon. After his funeral the letter was found and opened. It said:

To My Beloved Brother Pilots and Pals:

I go west, but with a cheerful heart. I hope what small sacrifice I have made may be of use to the cause.

When we fly we are damned fools, they say. When we are dead we weren't half-bad fellows. But everyone in this wonderful aviation service is doing the world far more good than the public can appreciate. We risk our necks; we give our lives; we perfect a service for the benefit of the world at large. They, mind you, are the ones who call us fools.

But stick to it, boys. I'm still very much with you all. See you all again.

= 6 =

THE AIRLINES ARE BORN

THE KELLY ACT OF 1925 was the brainchild of Representative Clyde Kelly, who felt that the Government should get out of the airmail business and let private operators assume the risks for whatever profit they could make. When the bill became law in February, 1925, the Post Office Department began the gradual process of closing down the Airmail Service. Advertisements were placed in newspapers asking for bids on eight airmail routes—only feeder lines at first, to enable the operators to gain experience.

The idea of having a private contractor fly the mail for pay was not a new one. The first contract had been issued to Edward Hubbard in 1919, and his flight became the first international airmail trip as he began service between Seattle, Washington, and Victoria, British Columbia, in a Boeing C-700 pontoon-equipped biplane on March 3rd that year. Operating as Hubbard Air Transport, he was awarded a permanent contract for the 74-mile route after a two-month probationary period and flew the Seattle run for the next seven years. He received $200 for each round trip.

Other small companies were awarded contracts similar to Hubbard's, but they were always for short routes. The Kelly Bill, also called the Airmail Act, was the needed stimulus to get contract mail flying started on a nation-wide basis.

The first five contracts were awarded by Postmaster General Harry J. New on October 7, 1925, but a man who was to receive a later contract was the first to put a contract route into operation. He was Henry Ford, the automobile maker, who for two years previously had been manufacturing an excellent new transport plane designed by William B. Stout. Months before bidding began on a mail contract, Ford Air Transport was operating with surprising regularity on routes from Detroit to Chicago and Cleveland. Consequently, it did not take Ford long to begin his contract airmail flying. The plane Stout designed was an all-metal monoplane embodying an abnormally thick internally-stressed wing and powered with a Liberty engine. In a later refinement it became the Ford Trimotor plane of enduring fame.

By the end of 1926 contract airlines were shuttling back and forth over twelve airmail routes. And in 1927 the transcontinental, or "Columbia," route was let in two segments, San Francisco – Chicago and Chicago – New York. These and other contract awards gave the United States a comprehensive airmail system and a firm basis for the magnificent all-purpose airlines now serving all the people.

Airmail brought in so much more revenue than did passengers that few of the contractors bothered to install seats in their planes. In fact, most of the mail planes were inadequate for passenger service, and it was only with the prodding of the Government that most mail routes became airlines capable of handling people as well as mail bags. This was brought about by Walter Folger Brown, a Postmaster General who envisioned an air network much like that in existence today. Mr. Brown was instrumental in getting Congress to change the method of payment to mail contractors. Where they had been collecting revenue on the weight of mail they carried, they were soon to be paid on the basis of the volume of space available for the mail. This encouraged them to buy larger airplanes that could carry passengers as well as goods.

One mail contractor, Western Air Express, with a mail contract route between Los Angeles and Salt Lake City, had tried from the very first to boost its mail income by carrying passengers, and in 1927 it received a grant from the Daniel Guggenheim Fund to buy modern passenger airplanes so that an intelligent study could be made of the potential in passenger traffic. The experiment was so successful that the grant was repaid within two years.

One of the most expensive ventures of the period was the formation of a transcontinental air-rail passenger service known as Transcontinental Air Transport (TAT), which was later to merge with several other airlines and become Transcontinental & Western Air (TWA), and still later, Trans World Airlines. This company was formed to prove that a luxury passenger service, utilizing train by night and plane by day, could succeed. The point was not well taken. TAT lost $2,750,000 in a year and a half. While passengers were potentially a good source of revenue, mail pay was an absolute necessity.

With airline operators dependent upon the Government for their very existence, the Postmaster General became the most powerful individual in civil aviation. This fact was not lost upon Walter Folger Brown, who was appointed to that post in 1929 by the newly-elected President, Herbert C. Hoover. Although his methods were severely attacked by many in the industry, Brown single-mindedly set out to build a broad airline network that would cover the country and become self-sufficient. It was his unswerving belief that the airlines should base their economy principally on passenger business so that government subsidy in the form of excess airmail payments could ultimately be withdrawn. When a new administration came in years later Brown became a figure of public debate, but there is no question that the power he wielded over the airlines was used to speed the formation of an efficient United States air transportation system.

Brown's job was simplified by the economic processes that overtook the many disparate contract airlines as they entered the boom days touched off by the Lindbergh flight from New York to Paris. Although some contract carriers made profits, many of them were consistently in the red, while others barely broke even. With the vast influx of capital into aviation in the late years of the 1920's, three principal holding companies were formed, each of them a giant composed of engine and aircraft manufacturers and operating airlines. Piece by piece they bought up large and small airplane operators, eliminating some, merging little lines into larger ones, and gradually giving shape to a highly competitive, yet geographically integrated, transportation system. Although today's airline system is utterly divorced from the manufacturing industry by law, there was nothing illegal or sinister about this process in the twenties.

In his studies of the United States map, Brown concluded that three transcontinental mail routes were needed, a northern, a central, and a southern route, to be augmented by smaller lines operating roughly north and south. With the addition of a more northerly fourth transcontinental route and a network of local service airlines, this is essentially the picture of the present-day airline system. By the time Brown was replaced in office by James A. Farley, he had accomplished his vision. In awarding new contracts, extending old routes, and using economic pressure to force mergers he considered desirable, Brown consistently favored those lines with the strongest financial backing. Thus, the systems controlled by the big holding companies were often favored over competitors, even though the independent lines sometimes offered lower bids for carrying the mail. This did not sit well with independent businessmen, whose capital and lives were wrapped up in their airlines. Many of them were doomed to go out of business for lack of mail contracts. Their resentment and opposition to Brown were at least partially responsible for the investigation that led to the cancellation by President Roosevelt of all airmail contracts in 1934.

Competition put a premium on economy of operation. Thus, operators shopped around for the most efficient airplanes they could buy, and manufacturers engaged in a contest to design aircraft to carry bigger loads faster and at less cost. As passenger transportation grew to larger proportions, safety became a predominating factor in design. Passengers expected a reasonable degree of schedule reliability, so means had to be found of extending the conditions under which safe flight could be accomplished. Each of these factors was a positive force in the evolution of the transport airplane.

Edward P. Warner, a noted scholar in aeronautics and then editor of the magazine *Aviation*, cited five engineering developments as the most important during the period, according to Henry Ladd Smith in the authoritative history of the airlines, *Airways*. These were: higher wing loads, the trend toward use of more than one engine, the NACA engine cowl, the appearance of high octane fuel, and internally braced wings.

Wing loading—the ratio of the plane's gross weight to the wing area—has an important bearing on the speed with which an engine can pull a plane through the air. The development of wing slots and flaps have accentuated this characteristic.

The use of two or more engines in an airplane is a safety measure as well as a means of increasing motive power. Modern aircraft can take off and climb on two of their four engines or one of their two engines. Performance of early multi-engine aircraft was not so impressive, but these aircraft did have a safety margin in case of the failure of one power plant.

The radial engine cowling designed by the National Advisory Committee for Aeronautics reduces engine drag by as much as half. Until Fred E. Weick developed the cowling—a kind of shell enveloping the engine—power plants were suspended, uncovered, under the wings. Use of the cowling increased speed

The first air express shipment, a bolt of cloth, was flown by Phil O. Parmalee from Dayton to Columbus, Ohio, in 1912. Above, Max Morehouse (left), the proprietor of a Columbus dry goods store, and A. Roy Knabenshue, one of the Wright brothers' pilots, pose for news photographers with the package.

and permitted designers to build engines into the wings and fuselages of the new aircraft.

High octane gasoline gives an engine greater efficiency and therefore reduces operating costs and either increases the airplane's range or its payload.

The wing stressed internally reduces drag. With the more recent development of stressed skin, the skin itself becomes part of its own supporting structure, rather than just a covering, and simplifies the internal construction.

All these developments and many more—such as the perfection of in-flight broadcasting, feathering propellers, retractable landing gear, and radio navigational devices—had a cumulative effect on airplane design and airline operating practices, so that each new model brought not only greater safety and speed to the nation's airways but also a higher degree of efficiency and economy to the airlines.

The first mail plane designed to carry passengers was so economical to fly in comparison with others of the mid-1920 vintage that its manufacturer, Boeing, won the longest contract route with a low bid. Boeing Air Transport, flying between Chicago and San Francisco, used the Boeing 40, a single-engine biplane with an open rear cockpit for the pilot and an enclosed cabin for two passengers between the wings. Primarily, of course, it was a mail plane, and many other manufacturers were soon turning out mail transports far more satisfactory than the DH's, which had been standard when Post Office pilots operated the routes in the first years of airmail.

The keen competition that has always existed among airlines led to the use of bigger and better passenger transports. By the first years of the 1930's, a variety of them were criss-crossing the country. The tri-motor Fokkers were high-wing monoplanes that enjoyed great popularity for a time but lost out to more advanced types in the early 1930's. The Stout plane, one of the early all-metal craft with the internally-stressed wing, evolved from a single Liberty-powered transport into a tri-motor craft using three 410-h.p. Pratt & Whitney Wasp radial power plants. Manufactured by Ford, it was known affectionately to pilots as the "tin goose." By 1929, 135 of them had been made and they were in use on such important lines as National Air Transport, TAT, Colonial Air Transport, Northwest Airways, and Maddux. American Airways and Eastern Air Transport favored the last of the big biplanes, the Curtiss Condor. The Condor, powered with two engines, was the first plane to be soundproofed and fitted with berths for passengers. Boeing brought out a 24-passenger tri-motor biplane for use on the United Air Lines route over the mountains of the West. It was bigger than any of them except the 32-passenger Fokker F-32, but proved to be enormously expensive to operate.

The first of the truly modern transport aircraft began to appear on the nation's airways in 1933, and within a few years the domestic airlines had standardized almost fully on three types. In comparison with their forerunners, they looked compact, racy, and powerful. The Boeing 247, the Lockheed Electra, and the Douglas DC-2 were all low-wing monoplanes, completely equipped for instrument flying and powered with two radial engines faired into the leading edge of the wing. They brought new standards of safety, comfort for passengers and crews, speed, and durability into air transportation. If airplanes could improve so much in such a short time, would it soon be possible to link foreign capitals to the United States by air? There were men who dared to think so and dared to try.

America's first foreign airmail contract (FAM I) went to an East Coast airline back in the 1920's, when Colonial Air Transport received permission to carry mail between New York and Montreal. Until the Pearl Harbor disaster brought the nation into World War II, the glamour line of American aviation had been the premier foreign airline—Pan-American Airways—which had argued, hacked, and flown its way from the United States down through South America, up into Alaska, across the Pacific to China, and across the Atlantic to Great Britain.

Hardy American pioneers who laid out the railroads and mountain highways were hardly more persevering and tolerant of hardships than the air-minded men who chopped their way through tropical jungles to lay out airports, who existed on lonely atolls to operate radio and weather stations, and who fought tetse flies and frostbite and ignorance and distrust to push the air frontiers outward from America.

By 1929, Pan-American Grace Airways (Panagra) was operating the longest international air route in the world between Miami and Montevideo, Uruguay. The route included stops in Cuba, Mexico, Nicaragua, Panama, Columbia, Peru, Chile, and Argentina.

One of the original pioneer pilots who flew the entire 7,300-mile route at one time or another was Robert C. Reeve, the late president of Reeve Aleutian Airways operating in Alaska. Reeve had been hired by the Ford Motor Company to pilot the new Ford Trimotor planes for potential buyers and delivered the first one to Peru for Panagra. Because of his experience, he was chosen to fly the newly-established Foreign Airmail Route 9 in 1929, which was a 1,900-mile stretch between Lima and Santiago—at this time the world's longest and fastest mail route and the longest air route in the world.

Reeve covered the 3,800-mile round trip twice a week and received the highest pay of any airline pilot at the time—$1,000 a month. Flying more than 150 hours a month, most of the time over 10,000 feet without oxygen, Reeve set several route speed records. However, these were not set by flying the Ford Trimotors; instead, Reeve chose a single-engine Fairchild monoplane which was "the best high altitude, high-load plane in the world at the time." In addition, Reeve was the first to fly a South American mail route at night over the treacherous Andes. Reeve described one of his record-setting flights:

I was at Buenos Aires waiting my turn to fly the mail on to Uruguay. A bad storm over the Andes had held up the westbound mail for over twenty-four hours so I volunteered to try to get through and make up for the lost time. I took off and flew straight through to Santiago over "the Hump" through the most violent weather I've ever experienced. The downdrafts and updrafts were so severe that I had a constant vision of mail, Fairchild and Reeve being splattered all over the mountain peaks below. I landed at Santiago and immediately gassed the plane for the next leg, north and up the coast.

The weather out of Santiago was typical—clear out over the Pacific but fog and low clouds over the shoreline up to the mountains. The Andes sticking up out of the clouds on my right were a constant reminder that I had a rough choice to make if the engine quit—ditch in the ocean, try to land on the side of a cliff or let down through the clouds to I knew not what.

I made two stops enroute to Lima and it was the same problem of trying to find the airport each time. The only way I could get in was to fly out over the Pacific where it was clear and let down to about a hundred feet above the water which was the base of the clouds. Then I would come in under the cloud layer and look for the airport. The field personnel had fires burning to help me find the place.

One thing that made the trip from Santiago north a little different on this trip was that it got dark after I left Santiago and I had to fly the entire coastal run in pitch darkness. I used a flashlight to read the compass so I could follow a reasonable course and stay between the water and the mountains.

I made the trip of nineteen hundred miles in twenty hours and the northbound mail got back on schedule. I didn't realize that I was setting a record or establishing an aviation "first." The mail had to go through or Panagra would have lost a little of its stature in the eyes of the Latins. Besides, I was flying mail for our government in those sacks marked "U.S. Mail." I guess I wanted to prove that Americans flying the mail outside the U.S. borders could do their jobs as well as those flying the domestic mail inside. Call it what you want but I felt that the honor of the United States was at stake, too, and I wasn't going to let it get tarnished without making an honest try.

There were no old, bold pilots flying the Panagra mail route. Those who were bold never lived to become old. The short, inadequately prepared fields, primitive servicing and living facilities, the 20,000-foot mountains, and the ever-present, death-dealing weather marked the route then and now as the roughest airmail route in the world.

In 1930, in spite of the tremendous hazards, Bob Reeve set a world record for airmail pilots which has never been equaled. He flew 1,476 hours of straight mail flying and never failed to meet his schedule. When asked his secret of survival, he answers simply, "I taught myself always to fly a little scared and I never let myself get into a flying situation where I didn't have an 'out.' "

Years later, when he pioneered Alaskan skies, the experience gained on the Panagra mail route kept Reeve alive on many occasions. The Aleutian weather, conceded by all pilots to be the worst in the world, was not bad enough to prevent Reeve from flying the mail over "the route nobody wants" on a scheduled basis from Anchorage to Attu. Reeve did not consider himself an airmail pioneer. "The real airmail pioneers," he said, "are the men who flew the domestic routes in their beat-up DH-4's for the Post Office Department between 1918 and 1927. I am a second-generation airmail pilot because I flew for an established airline. Today's pilots are third-generation pilots because, although they fly the mail, they don't know they have it on board."

While Reeve and his brother Panagra pilots were pioneering the Latin-American routes, Pan-American sent staffs out to Hawaii, Midway, Wake and Guam Islands, the Philippines, and the Orient to set up a tenuous airway across the vast Pacific. In November, 1935, when the domestic airline system was trying to recover from the disastrous mail cancellations the year before, the first flight took off, to start regular trans-Pacific service. By 1939 this company was operating regular passenger, mail, and cargo service to Great Britain. So far as the United States was concerned, the ocean air routes had been Pan-American's up to this point, and hardly anybody had raised an objection. But in 1940 a second carrier, American Export Airlines, received a temporary certificate of convenience and necessity to link America with Europe. Transoceanic flying had hardly been lush business, but the European war made it attractive. Pan-Am's empire was to grow, rather than diminish, but it would become only one of many American ocean air carriers.

In the process of swallowing larger ocean draughts with each step forward, Pan-American stimulated the development of a remarkable series of flying boats by a group of manufacturers, culminating in the spectacular Boeing Clippers that maintained the Atlantic service. Igor Sikorsky, who will be remembered as the manufacturer of the first multi-engine plane, turned out a progression of large and comfortable flying boats for Pan-Am

Robert C. Reeve, famous Alaskan bush pilot, stands beside a Lockheed Vega in South America. He flew the world's longest airmail route for Pan American Airways between Lima, Peru, and Santiago, Chile, during the 1930s. He covered the 3,800-mile round-trip twice a week and received the highest pay of any airline pilot in the world at the time—$1,000 per month.

and later, for its rival, Amex. Glenn L. Martin, who started manufacturing aircraft in 1909, provided the airline with other spacious boats of long range and high capacity. Consolidated, which also supplied NYRBA, Pan-Am's principal South American rival at one time, developed its commercial models into the famous Catalina patrol boats of World War II and more recent fame. Flying boats, unlike landplanes which are restricted to the runway lengths of their airports, can be built big because waterways offer immense landing and take-off runs. Their boat hulls give them a roominess that landplane designers can only dream of. Pan-Am's standards of comfort for passengers in prewar days were therefore designed to help compensate for the very high fares.

Under their government airmail contracts many domestic airlines flew regularly over ocean routes, and in some cases, did a bit of pioneering in the process. For instance, Howard Hall, a

TWA pilot flying the Atlantic, conceived the idea of pressure pattern flying, a method of deviating from great circle routes to take advantage of winds that follow a circular pattern around high and low pressure areas. With the Army Air Force's permission, Hall first experimented with the method in the winter of 1943-44, and soon he was joined by American Airlines and Army Air Force experimental crews. The result was that soon all airplanes were able to fly westbound direct across the North Atlantic, instead of following a three- to five-day route down through Africa, across the South Atlantic, and up to the United States. This method is used today by all transoceanic airlines.

Many of the domestic carriers put in their requests with the government for foreign routes to be operated commercially once the war was ended. A great struggle ensued over single airline versus controlled competition on world air routes. The latter group won out. Shortly after World War II Pan-American became just one of many United States airlines—but still the largest—to carry the flag and the mail to foreign lands.

The growth of the airlines since World War II is well known and cannot be covered here. The prop-driven aircraft have been replaced by fast jets that have compressed the time zones of the world so much that passengers find it difficult to adjust to the time differences. The supersonic transports tighten the time factor even more.

While mail and passengers have benefited from the growth of the airlines, so has the transport of things by air prospered—"air express," as we have decided to name the transport of cargo by aircraft.

The airlines began carrying express packages shortly after winning their first airmail contracts. Cargo haulage began on a large scale during World War II and blossomed forth into big business shortly afterward. All the airlines now carry freight, and most of them have planes fitted especially for cargo to the exclusion of passengers. Today every conceivable object that can be fitted into an airplane has been transported by air. And there seems to be no limit to the growth of this airline "bonus" business, either. Ever since Phil O. Parmalee flew a bolt of silk from Dayton to Columbus, Ohio, in a Wright biplane in 1912, the growth curve has been ever upward. The value of this bolt of cloth was $1,000 and weighed 60 pounds. Today, tons of cargo are being carried around the globe every minute of every day and the value is in the millions. Almost eight decades have passed since the idea was first conceived to ship express cargo by air. It has survived the acid tests of time and the marketplace to find unquestioned acceptance as one of the world's most valued commercial institutions.

While the growth of aviation has been steady when measured over the years since the airlines first flew the mails in the late 1920's, there was a dark period in this growth. Just as the Army Air Service pilots had proved the feasibility of flying the mail on regular schedules in 1918, Army Air Corps pilots were called upon to keep the service going. The year was 1934—a year that interrupted the progress of the airlines. It was also a year that proved that a nation needed airpower for its survival.

=7=

CRITICAL MONTHS: THE ARMY TAKES OVER

THE KELLY ACT OF 1925 was actually entitled "An Act to Encourage Commercial Aviation and to Authorize the Postmaster General to Contract for Airmail Service." Its purpose was not only to speed the delivery of mail, but to encourage American capital to invest in what could be an entirely new industry. Accordingly, it was believed that commercial aviation in the United States could best be helped through the operation of airmail routes by American citizens and corporations, using aircraft manufactured exclusively in the United States. To apply for the route contracts, individuals had to prove that they were American citizens, and corporations had to show that at least 75 percent of the capital stock was owned by American citizens. In addition, each aircraft had to qualify for an airworthiness certificate and each pilot had to be able to produce a "certificate of fitness."

The first contracts specified that contractors would be paid at a rate not to exceed four-fifths of the revenue derived from airmail. However, this presented great problems of checking the mail and calculating the amounts due each airline. Employees were confused and the excessive handling tended to slow down the movement of the mails. As a consequence, beginning on July 1, 1926, the basis for payment was a fixed rate per pound of mail.

As the contractors began to operate according to the rules, it was found that the public was still not used to the idea of sending letters by air. Something unusual in the way of focusing public attention on flying the mail was needed. It was found in May,

1927, when Charles A. Lindbergh, a young airmail pilot, on the Chicago – St. Louis run, made his famous flight from New York to Paris. In one month's time, there was a 20 percent increase in the poundage of mail carried on contract routes. Most, if not all, of this increase was attributed to the additional interest in the use of airmail service created by Lindbergh's remarkable feat and the publicity given to aviation in general on his return from Paris.

There is no doubt that the years 1927 and 1928 marked the greatest boom era in aviation up to that time. Lindbergh's tour of the country, sponsored by the Daniel Guggenheim Fund for the Promotion of Aeronautics, urging cities and towns to establish airports and pointing out the rapid growth and potential of commercial air transportation to each community, had a far-reaching effect on the growth of contract mail service. Airports sprang up all over the country, and the Post Office Department was beseiged with petitions and delegations requesting the establishment of airmail service through their communities.

By 1931, passenger hauling by the contract airmail carriers had become fully accepted. Increased use of radio communication between plane and ground had taken place, and the Post Office Department now required that contractors procure airplanes capable of cruising at least 140 miles per hour. By July 1, 1933, 23 airmail routes had been established with a combined length of 27,735 miles. During that month, 644,172 pounds of mail were carried along with 47,398 paying passengers and 112,666 pounds of air express packages.

While the statistics seemed impressive, the apparently healthy commercial air industry was in trouble. As early as 1932 there had been agitation for the cancellation of the contracts made in 1930. A Congressional hearing had been held, and it was found that some contracts and route certificates had been awarded without public advertisement. Accusations were made that public funds were being wasted because contracts had been let to favored companies to the disadvantage of the American taxpayer. The "airmail scandal" became a hot political issue at the end of the Hoover Administration when a business depression gripped the country.

Senator Hugo Black of Alabama, Senate leader at the time the Roosevelt Administration was seated, accused the former Republican Postmaster General Walter F. Brown and the airlines of collusion and fraud. In the House of Representatives, the Crane Committee reported that interlocking interests and directorates among the aircraft companies and the airlines had defin-

Many types of Army Air Corps aircraft were pressed into airmail service between February and June, 1934, after all commercial airmail contracts were cancelled. A Douglas B-7 bomber flies over Salt Lake City area, Utah.

itely prevented the free development of aviation and concurred that public funds had been wasted. The Congressional investigations alleged that the airmail appropriations had been used to favor a few corporations, that the Postmaster General had avoided public bidding, and that from July, 1930, through December, 1933, airmail contractors had received more than $78,000,000 from the Government, although actual service rendered was only about 40 percent of that amount.

While Postmaster General Brown had answers for the accusations made against him, there was grave doubt that he had acted in the public interest. The whole affair reached a climax on February 9, 1934, when President Roosevelt ordered Postmaster General James A. Farley to cancel all airmail contracts.

Major General Benjamin D. Foulois, Chief of the Army Air Corps, was in his Washington office on the morning of February 9th where he received a telephone call from Second Assistant

Postmaster General Harllee Branch. Would General Foulois drop over to Branch's office to chat about some aviation matters? Foulois replied that he would be glad to.

On the way to Branch's office from the Munitions Building, the peppery Foulois wondered what Branch wanted. He had recently been appointed to serve with Branch and Eugene Vidal of the Department of Commerce on an interdepartmental committee for aviation policy and assumed that he was going to discuss some ideas about the national airways that they were hoping to improve or future air commerce legislation.

Foulois had been following the airmail scandals in the papers but assumed that if the contracts with the airlines were cancelled, the mail would just go by train until the matter was straightened out. This feeling was confirmed when Foulois found that Branch wanted to talk about the airmail runs, schedules, and alternatives if the mail wasn't flown, and internal management problems they had encountered in handling airmail.

The two men were relaxed and chatted for over an hour. Branch mentioned the possibility of the airmail contracts being cancelled and casually asked, "Benny, if the President should cancel all contracts with civilian carriers, could the Air Corps carry the mail to keep the system going?"

Foulois thought a moment before answering. The country was in a deep depression, and the Air Corps had suffered badly from lack of appropriations to buy new planes, train pilots, build up-to-date facilities, and conduct research. The Air Corps had no cargo equipment, and none of the pilots had ever flown over regular routes on instruments or at night. Their planes were simply not equipped for such an operation.

Still, Foulois thought, maybe this was an opportunity to focus attention on military aviation. The pilots would get some badly needed training which had been curtailed drastically because of the shortage of funds to buy gasoline, ground equipment, and spare parts.

"We could do it, Mr. Branch, if the President wanted us to try," Foulois answered.

"How much time would you need to get ready, Ben?"

"About a week or ten days, I would guess," Foulois replied, not realizing the impact that such an informal answer to a casual question would have. Although he didn't know it, the time to get ready was beginning *at that very moment!*

Foulois returned to his office and called his staff together to ask them to work up some contingency plans just in case the Army might someday be called on to fly the mails. Once he

A Douglas B-7 is located at Reno, Nevada. Pilot (with goggles) is Capt. B.E. Mouton.

approved their plans, he would submit them through channels to General Douglas MacArthur, Army Chief of Staff.

Before he could finish briefing his staff, he was called to MacArthur's office. When Foulois closed the door, MacArthur got right to the point. "Foulois, a newsman told me that the President just released an Executive Order giving the Air Corps the job of flying the mail ten days from now. What do you know about it?"

Foulois gulped and explained that he had just had a conference with the Second Assistant Postmaster General but that nothing definite had been decided upon.

"That's what you think," MacArthur answered, scowling. "But, that's academic now. The question is, can you do the job?"

"Yes, sir, we can," Foulois replied. "That is, if the President will see that we get what we need in the way of support—moral as well as material. It won't be any picnic, but I think we can do it."

MacArthur smiled and said, "O.K., Benny, you're on your own. Yell when you need help from me and keep me informed."

In the next forty-eight hours, Foulois and his staff met in continuous session to organize and plan for the task. There was urgency now because Postmaster General Farley telegraphed all private airmail contractors that all contracts were "hereby cancelled, effective midnight, February 19, 1934."

The decision was quickly reached that the Air Corps should not operate over all the routes that had been flown by the airlines. Instead, the cities in which the Federal banks were located would be connected so that the use of the airmail by commercial banks would not suffer. Therefore, the Air Corps would operate over 12 routes instead of the 26 flown by the airlines.

The route structure was divided into three zones, and Major B.Q. Jones, Lieutenant Colonel Horace M. Hickman, and Lieutenant Colonel Henry H. "Hap" Arnold were placed in charge of the Eastern, Central, and Western Zones. Two hundred officers, 324 enlisted men, and 122 planes of all types—pursuit, attack, bombardment, and observation—were alerted and assigned stations from which to begin operations. The baggage compartments of the attack and pursuit planes were modified where possible to get more mail-sack space. The bomb bays of the bombers were sealed. Radios and instruments were installed in as many of the planes as possible.

But, while Foulois was laying careful plans, he was deeply concerned. Only a small number of Army pilots had had any extensive night flying experience, and even fewer knew anything about instrument flying. The reason was simple: no equipment. Very few Air Corps planes were equipped with landing, navigation, or cockpit lights. Only airliners had the new gyro instruments, and the newly-developed radio beam flying techniques had been developed by the airline pilots—not the Army. Without instruments or radios, they had no way to practice.

By February 16th, Air Corps pilots were making familiarization flights along their respective routes without mail. That night, Foulois received bad news. Two fatal crashes had occurred that day in the Western Zone. Lieutenants J.D. Grenier and Edwin D. White had crashed to their deaths in a snowstorm on a flight in an A-12 between Cheyenne and Salt Lake City. Lieutenant James Y. Eastham, flying a B-7, had crashed near Jerome, Idaho, at night in a fog.

The bad weather that had contributed to both crashes was a prelude of worse to come. By noon on the 19th, snow, fog, and rain had moved into the Eastern Zone and grounded everything.

Mail is loaded aboard a twin-engine Martin B-10 bomber at Burbank, California.

A blizzard whipsawed through the Western Zone. The only Army flights that began their routes on schedule were those in the South and Midwest. However, as the weather abated, schedules were met and things started to go smoothly.

It wasn't long before Foulois received more tragic news. On February 22nd, Lieutenant Durnwald O. Lowry, flying an Eastern Zone route, crashed south of Toledo, Ohio, and was killed. His was the first fatality with mail aboard. That same day, Lieutenant H.L. Dietz, flying from Washington to New York, became lost in fog and heavy rain at night over Maryland. He circled over the town of Marion Station until local citizens drove to a pasture and lit up a "runway" with their headlights. Dietz struck the top of a tree on the final approach, and his plane was flipped sideways and crashed into a telephone pole. Dietz was knocked unconscious but survived.

Just after these reports were received, Foulois learned that Lieutenant Fred J. Patrick had been killed near Denison, Texas, while en route to supervise pilots on the Midwest runs. He carried no mail and was alone.

Weather had been a major factor in each of these accidents. Underlying causes, no doubt, were the lack of proper instruments and radio equipment and the pilot's inexperience in blind flying.

The newspapers, sympathizing with the commercial airlines that had lost their contracts, publicized the accidents mercilessly and criticized Foulois severely. To make matters worse, on February 23rd, a plane ferrying a group of pilots to their duty station was forced down off a New York beach. Lieutenant George F. McDermott, one of the passengers, could not swim and drowned. The newspapers immediately continued their blast at Foulois and condemned "those airmail murders" and the "needless slaughter of brave airmen." Ironically, on the same day, an airliner crashed in Utah killing eight people, and little mention was made of this tragedy in any newspaper anywhere.

The criticism of Foulois and the Roosevelt Administration was politically inspired and fostered by the airlines that had lost their contracts. Foulois and his pilots could only continue to do their best. Restrictions were placed on night and instrument flying, and supervisory personnel were required to personally certify that all planes under their jurisdiction were equipped properly for each flight. Planes without lights, radios, or instruments were prohibited from flights at night or into known instrument conditions.

Many leading newspapers representing Republican interests continued their attacks on the Army Air Corps and the tough little fighter who ran it. Foulois received permission to go on a national radio hookup and explain his views. He told the author:

> I began my talk by reviewing how the Air Corps had been given the task of flying the mail and how I had organized our resources to do the job. I then explained that our planes were being rapidly equipped with radio receivers and told how radio beams worked on the airways.
>
> I did not deny that we had serious handicaps to overcome but I pointed out that, with all the ruckus raised about "legalized murder," only one death had occurred on a scheduled airmail run. I closed my statement by urging the public to give the Army mail pilots their loyal support.

Army Air Corps mail routes are discussed by Capt. Ross G. Hoyt (left) and Major Carl Spaatz when the Army Air Corps flew the mail during the winter of 1934.

The personal message from Foulois did little good. Newspaper editorials condemned him for being so callous and inhumane that he could condemn gallant American youths to their deaths in "flaming coffins." He was accused of having joined the Democratic Administration bandwagon and being a political pawn.

As if this continued harassment were not enough, Foulois had other troubles. He had been assured that adequate funds would be transferred from the Post Office Department to the Air Corps to pay the expenses of the Army operation. They were not. As a result pilots and mechanics, living under poor conditions far from their regular stations, were not paid any per diem and were having a rough go making ends meet. Enlisted men on low pay suffered most of all. Many were only earning $17 per month and had no bank accounts to fall back on. They lived in the hangars and existed on handouts from the pilots or local townspeople.

Other problems plagued the operation. Supplies were not delivered to the various control points on time. Tools were not available, the makeshift maintenance shacks were inadequate, and work was done in the open in howling blizzards or drenching rains.

The plight of the men soon became apparent and, as Foulois hoped, public attention was gradually focused where it belonged—on the pitiful state of equipment of the Air Corps. New bombers, Martin B-10's, began coming off the production line and could be used to replace the pursuit and observation planes that were inadequate for the mail-hauling job. The pay situation improved, and supplies started going where they were needed.

But the feeling of better days ahead was short-lived. On the night of March 9th, Lieutenant Otto Wienecke, flying an O-39, crashed near Burton, Ohio, during a heavy snowstorm. That same night, a mechanic, Sergeant Ernest C. Sell, was killed in the crash of a twin-engine B-6 just after take-off from Dayton, Florida. The pilot and another passenger were unhurt.

As if two tragedies were not enough for one night, Lieutenant Colonel "Hap" Arnold wired Foulois that Lieutenants Frank L. Howard and Arthur R. Kerwin had been killed on a night take-off from Cheyenne, Wyoming. The cause of these three accidents was never fully ascertained.

On the morning of March 10th, General Foulois was ordered to the White House. Accompanied by General MacArthur, he was escorted to the President's bedroom, where the most famous man in the country lay propped up in bed.

MacArthur introduced Foulois, but the introduction was ignored. Scowling deeply, Roosevelt blurted out, "General, when are these airmail killings going to stop?"

Foulois promptly replied, "Only when airplanes stop flying, Mr. President."

Roosevelt stared at the diminutive Foulois through his pincenez glasses. Then began a ten-minute tongue lashing of both MacArthur and Foulois, the like of which Foulois had never received in his 35 years of military service. He received no guidance, and the two military men left the White House with heads bowed.

Foulois asked for a ten-day "stand down" period and reduced routes. Both requests were granted. Operations were to resume on March 19th; in the meantime, pilots were to practice night and instrument flying and transition into newer planes. Two days before operations were to resume, Lieutenant R.G. Richardson was killed on a training flight near Cheyenne.

The operations were resumed on March 19th, and the future looked brighter. New B-10's were coming into the inventory almost daily. Pilots were being ordered to go through an instrument training course. But again the optimism was interrupted

Army Air Corps trainers were used on the low-altitude routes east of Denver.

by another fatal crash. On March 30th, Lieutenant Thurman A. Wood, flying an old A-12, was approaching DeWitt, Iowa, at night. He flew into a severe thunderstorm and in trying to reverse his course, lost control and spun in. The cause, apparently, was like most of the others—the lethal combination of night and instrument conditions coupled with pilot inexperience and inadequate instruments.

In the weeks that Foulois had been fighting his problems, plans were under way to open negotiations for new contracts, and it appeared certain that commercial operators would resume the routes. At the end of April, Foulois was instructed to phase out all his operations by mid-May. Air Corps pilots ceased flying all of the routes except one by May 17th. On June 1st, the last bag of mail was flown between Chicago and Fargo, North Dakota, by an Army plane, and the books were closed on a tragic but vitally important chapter in the history of American aviation.

DAILY AIR MAIL OPERATIONS
STATION, CHEYENNE
DATE 4-21-34

EAST BOUND	ARR	DEP
TRIP 2	1730	1800
" 4	0930	1000
" 6	1045	1115

WEST BOUND	ARR	DEP
TRIP 1	1515	1530
" 3	0000	0525
" 5	245	315

AIRPLANE TYPE & NUMBER	PILOT	ARRIVED FROM	TIME	DEPARTED FOR	TIME	IN OUT SYMBOL	WT. OF MAIL TAKEN OFF	WT. OF MAIL PUT ON	TRIP NO. OR CASUAL NO.	DATE	REMARKS
A-12 33-236	Mock	OH	0505cs	CX	0125cs	NA NA 0310 0325	17pch 1pc 552#		3	1 20	✓
A-12 33-220	Rogers	OH	0700	CX	0325cs	NA NA 0515 0525	20pcks 589#		3	2 20	✓
O-35 31-315	McDaniel	CX	0945AS	SL	0630MS	OON K-1 0825		39pch 1pc 905#	2	20	✓
		Cancelled at depot consolidated with T1-2 1st							5		
A12 245	Backus	OH		CX	1215cs		17pcks 215#		5 5	21	
B-10	Stephenson	SL	845MS	CX	0630MS	OON RCT 0230MS	962#		1 1		
A12 33-231	Brown	CX		OH	820	NA NA 847 ASS		11pch 1pc 473#	4 4	20 20	✓ ✓
B-10 15	Bowman	SL	1000MT	CX	0745MS		249#		6	21	✓
M12 220	Gibner	CX		OH	1201 CF			11pch 261#	6	21 1pch N.Q wgt 2#	
									2		
								5 pcks 56#	3		
O-19 31-544	(Alpert)	CX	0720MS	DDE	06 25MS						✓

Air Corps airmail operations status boards at various locations indicated types of aircraft, pilots' names, schedule, and weight of mail carried.

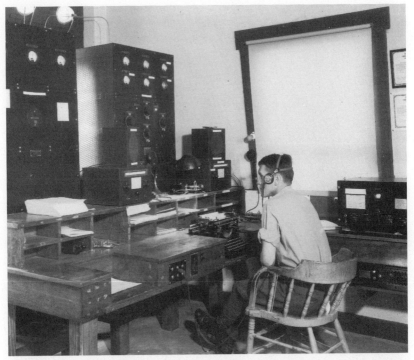

The Air Corps radio stations along the mail routes were manned by enlisted men of the Army Signal Corps. This station was located at Las Vegas, Nevada.

Postmaster General Farley, realizing that Foulois had borne the brunt of criticism he did not deserve, sent him a letter of praise and predicted that "the country and the Congress will, without doubt, give a more adequate support to the Army, will see to it that it has the most modern equipment obtainable and that sufficient funds are provided for the flyers to have the additional hours of flying which have so long been needed."

Farley also noted that "not a single pound of mail was lost during the time the Army had flown the mail."

The Air Corps did not receive any other words of praise, but the pilots and ground personnel who worked so long and hard under the most difficult conditions short of war had accomplished much. Over 13,000 hours of flying time had been logged, and pilots had flown over 1,500,000 miles carrying 777,000 pounds of mail. They had set a number of speed records over their routes and had learned many valuable lessons about operating aircraft on schedules.

Operations office and pilots' tents at Las Vegas, Nevada, during 1934 when the U.S. Army Air Corps flew the mail.

But it was their failures, not their successes, that were important. The crashes and deaths had pointed out as nothing else could in peacetime that the United States had a military air arm that was dangerously inadequate compared to those of other nations. In the months and years ahead, the tax-paying public gradually began to support military aviation. The planes that were placed on the drawing boards in the late 1930's were the planes that fought and won the war of the 1940's. As Foulois reminisced years later, "Flying the mail was a godsend for the Air Corps and the country. Without it, I am convinced we would have never recovered from the disaster at Pearl Harbor."

While the three-month experience had helped the Air Corps, it had also helped the airlines. The old routes were thrown open for bid, and when the new contracts were awarded, the nation had an air transportation system with a new look. Some old companies lost out on the bidding, and some new ones, built out of the remnants of old ones, were established and added new names to American history.

The basic pattern has changed little to this day. New routes have been granted and extensions given; parallel awards have been made to stimulate competition between cities or to provide enough service to handle heavy traffic demands; local service lines have been established. Passenger service has become paramount, but where passengers go, so goes the mail.

In the half-century of airmail service, the fondest dreams of those early airmail pioneers have been realized. Mail is now measured in tons instead of pounds and speed in Mach numbers instead of miles per hour. The original couriers of the clouds did their job well. We owe our aviation progress to their improvisations and cut-and-try experiments. We owe them our thanks for giving birth to the airline industry. More than that, we owe them our lives for giving us the basis for military airpower that won air supremacy at a time of national peril.

=== 8 ===

AIRMAIL FIRSTS

THE FIRST AIRMAIL FLIGHT sanctioned by a government postal system in an aircraft of any type took place on September 9, 1911, when Gustave Hamel carried a mail pouch from Hendon, near London, to Windsor Castle—a distance of 20 miles. It was two weeks later that Earle Ovington was sworn in as Airmail Pilot No. 1 in the United States and flew in a Bleriot monoplane with the first bag of United States Airmail in his lap.

But Hamel and Ovington were not the first to carry a letter from point to point by airplane. This honor belongs to Glenn Curtiss, a self-taught mechanic who built planes that competed with the early Wright models. On May 1, 1910, he had flown one of his own planes on what was the most spectacular distance flight in American aviation up to that time.

Taking off from a pasture near Albany, New York, he flew to Poughkeepsie, then to Inwood via the Military Academy at West Point, and on to New York City to complete the first long-distance flight in the Western Hemisphere. He had covered 142$^{1}/_{2}$ miles in 2 hours and 50 minutes of flying time to win a $10,000 prize from the *New York World*. After landing, he presented a letter to Mayor William J. Gaynor of New York which had been given to him by the Mayor of Albany. While not an *official* airmail flight, it was the first recorded instance where a pilot of a heavier-than-air machine had carried written correspondence from one person to another.

Another "first" was the first official airmail flight by a woman pilot. Her name was Katherine Stinson, and she was a member of an illustrious flying family which included her brother Eddie and her sister Marjory. While teenagers, the Stinsons built and flew their own gliders. Katherine soloed at the age of 21 and then took part in many flying exhibitions.

It was at the Montana State Fair in 1913 that Katherine Stinson performed her airmail "first." She made daily flights at the fair, and as an added attraction it was proposed that she cary airmail pouches from the fair grounds and drop them to the postmaster in downtown Helena. She was properly sworn in by postmaster George W. Lanstrom, and the route designation 663002 was issued for this first airmail route in Montana and the West.

Katherine Stinson carried 1,333 post cards and letters on these daily trips. However, this was not her only airmail "first." In 1918, she persuaded the Post Office Department to put her on a regular mail run from Washington to Philadelphia. On September 26, 1918, she took off behind regular mail pilot Maurice Newton who led her to Philadelphia so she wouldn't get lost. The two returned the next day. To the chagrin of the Airmail Service pilots, especially Newton, the headline in a Washington paper that evening read: KATHERINE STINSON, FIRST AIRMAIL AVIATRIX, BEATS VETERAN NEWTON TO WASHINGTON. This was her third and last official airmail flight.

One of the airmail experiments conceived during the early days of the heavier-than-air flying machine was the delivery of mail by air to or from a ship at sea. The first pilot who planned to deliver mail from an outgoing ship back to land was J.A.C. McCurdy, who was scheduled to fly from the deck of the German ship *Kaiserin Augusta Victoria* on November 4, 1910. After the ship was fifty miles out of New York harbor, McCurdy was to fly a mail bag containing letters from the passengers to New York City for further dispatch to other destinations.

Special envelopes, inscribed "Aeroplane Mail, Hamburg America Line at Sea, Via Air Route to United States," were printed and sold to philatelists several days before the scheduled flight. However, during a last-minute engine check before loading the plane aboard the ship, the wooden propeller split and the flight was cancelled. But, since a large number of letters had been received, the mail was handled as if it had been flown; actually it was sent back by the pilot boat after the ship cleared the New York harbor.

Another flight was planned to take place to or from the *America* of the Hamburg-America line on the trip leaving New York on January 6, 1911. If the weather were unfavorable for the flight from the ship after leaving New York, the pilot, Hugh

Airmail pick up pilot Tom Kincheloe (right) and Ed Lowden, flight mechanic, pose beside an All-American Aviation Stinson Reliant aircraft. Pick up pilots were required to have a minimum of 4,000 flying hours and 10 years experience to be hired. Mechanics needed an aircraft and engine mechanic license. All flying personnel had to be natives of the area over which they were to fly.

Robinson, planned to have his "hydroplane" hoisted aboard upon arrival with the outgoing mail. Then, one hundred and fifty miles from the mouth of the Elbe River on arrival at the European end of the journey, his plane was to be put into the water and the mail destined for Europe flown to the harbor at Hamburg.

Robinson never made his trip either, for reasons not clear. And it was not until 1927 that a successful ship-to-shore flight was finally accomplished. On July 31st, Clarence D. Chamberlin sailed from New York on the *Leviathan* with his plane lashed to the deck. Next day, he flew it from the ship with 916 letters aboard and successfully completed his mission.

In 1928, a similar flight was planned from the deck of the S.S. *Conte Grande* when it arrived off Spain. The plane landed safely and mail postmarked in New York was delivered to Barcelona. On August 8th, that same year, a plane was catapulted from the *Ile de France* when it neared New York. This plane also landed safely and thus brought mail to New York a full eighteen hours ahead of the ship's arrival.

The Germans brought catapult mail to a high point of efficiency in the early thirties. The ships *Bremen, Europa,* and *Columbus* of the North German Lloyd Line were equipped with catapults and mail was delivered eighteen to twenty-four hours ahead of the ships at both ends of their runs. Experiments were also conducted with flying outgoing mail to the ships many hours after their departure, but the requirement to stop the ships and hoist the planes aboard caused insurmoutable problems. Thus, the delivery of mail to ships never passed the experimental stage.

The navies of the world have used planes to deliver mail to and from ships since carrier operations and sea planes were made safe. However, these flights were never recognized by philatelists as "official." Thus, Clarence D. Chamberlin is credited as the first man in airmail history to successfully complete a ship-to-shore flight with mail aboard. It is not known who deserves the credit as being the first to deliver mail to a ship at sea by air.

In the 1920's when distance, speed, and endurance records were being assaulted on an almost daily basis, mail was included on many flights which had national or international interest. The first trans-Atlantic mail flight, however, took place in June, 1919, when Captain John Alcock and Lieutenant Arthur W. Brown made the first non-stop flight across the Atlantic and captured the *Daily Mail* prize of 10,000 pounds. They

A Stinson Reliant makes a mail pick up at one of the 55 points on the All-American Aviation routes. The routes covered 845 miles over rough terrain in Ohio, Pennsylvania, and West Virginia.

left St. John's, Newfoundland, June 14, 1919, in a British-made Vickers-Vimy twin-engine bomber and landed at Clifden, Ireland, 16 hours later. To lighten wind resistance and reduce the total load, Alcock and Brown had constructed the landing gear so it could be dropped off after takeoff. Their landing in Ireland, therefore, was a rough one. The plane's nose plowed up a wide swath in the mud, and the propellers were smashed. The mail, however, was undamaged.

A month after this flight, a British airship, the R-34, crossed the Atlantic between July 2 and July 6, 1919, to become the first lighter-than-air craft to make the crossing. It made the

3,130-mile flight from East Fortune, Scotland, to Roosevelt Field, Long Island, in 108 hours elapsed time. A package of 14 letters was carried, and for reasons never fully explained, was dropped near the village of Selwar, Nova Scotia, during the trip. The package was not found until four months later.

The first London-to-Australia flight, the longest ever made by an air vehicle up to that time, was also made in 1919, between November 12th and December 10th. It was the first in a long series of annual races between the two countries. There were four entrants, all of whom carried mail for delivery to Australian addresses. Captain Ross Smith and his brother, Lieutenant Keith M. Smith, won the race and established another airmail "first." Their flight, flown in a converted Vickers-Vimy bombing plane resembling the one flown by Alcock and Brown, won for them a prize of $50,000 offered by the Australian government for making the distance in less than a month.

The two brothers left London with 500 gallons of gas and a week's supply of food. They encountered many dangers along the way but survived them all. Near Surabaya, Java, their plane was mired in a swamp, and take-off was possible only after a bamboo mat runway had been laid down. Near Calcutta, India, a large hawk smashed one of their propellers.

The brothers were both knighted in recognition of their achievement. They had flown the 11,060 miles from London to Port Darwin in Northern Australia in 27 days and 20 hours of elapsed time.

The first flights by airplane over the Arctic regions toward the North Pole were conducted by Roald Amundsen and Lincoln Ellsworth during the months of May and June, 1925. To defray expenses, "subscription postal cards" were issued to those contributing. They were addressed to the Trans-Polar Flights Expedition, Christiana, Norway. Although neither of the Dornier-Wal flying boats, the N-24 and N-25, reached the North Pole, the postal cards they carried are highly prized today.

After their attempt to reach the North Pole by airplane had failed, Amundsen and Ellsworth concluded that the dirigible was a better vehicle for polar travel because it could remain aloft for longer periods. In May, 1925, the two men left Rome, Italy, in the airship *Norge*. Seventy hours after casting off from Spitsbergen, Norway, the 16 men and one dog aboard completed an aerial voyage of incredible distance. They had flown over the North Pole and landed safely on the snow at Teller, Alaska, an Eskimo village of 55 inhabitants, after flying 3,300 miles through Arctic storms.

A Kellett autogyro piloted by John M. Miller takes off from the roof of the Philadelphia Post Office for the short flight to Philadelphia Airport in the late 1930s. Autogyros, unlike helicopters, needed a short takeoff run. The large rotor blades were not connected to an engine.

A total of 91 letters had been transported from Rome, Italy, to Teller and had received the postal circular cancellation "Teller, Alaska, A.M., May 13, 1926." To document the fact that these letters were genuine, five members of the crew made a sworn affidavit in Milan when they returned home stating that "we guarantee that besides the aforementioned letters, there exists no other correspondence transported by the *Norge* from Rome to Alaska, that is to say, they have completed the entire flight over the Pole."

In June, 1927, Commander Richard E. Byrd of the United States Navy wanted to fly the Atlantic in the Fokker monoplane *America*. With Bernt Balchen as chief pilot, George Noville, Bert Acosta, and Byrd left Roosevelt Field, New York, on June 29th. The flight ended disastrously on the beach at Ver-Sur-Mer, France, 42 hours later when the plane ran out of gas. Fortunately, injuries to the four men aboard were minor.

A few days before Byrd began his flight he was sworn in as an airmail pilot, which gave him the honor of being the first American to officially carry United States mail across the ocean in an airplane.

Since the Atlantic had been spanned, some intrepid pilots turned their attention to the Pacific. Captain Charles Kingsford-Smith, an Australian pilot, with Keith V. Andridson as copilot and Charles P.T. Ulm and William A. Todd as navigators, left Oakland, California, on May 31, 1928, for Australia. Flying a Fokker tri-motor, they made stops at Honolulu, the Fiji Islands, and Sydney before arriving at Brisbane. This spectacular flight of 7,400 miles was covered in 83 hours, 15 minutes flying time. Fifteen hundred letters were carried, which made another aviation and airmail "first."

One of the most difficult airmail route pioneering flights ever made took place when Alan J. Cobham, a leading British aviator, blazed an aerial trail from London to Cape Town, South Africa. Two attempts to span the length of the Dark Continent had been made in 1920, but the heat and the dangers of the jungle had spelled disaster for both flights.

Captain Cobham had been selected by Imperial Airways, Ltd., to make an experimental flight for the opening of a passenger and mail route to connect England with her far-flung colonies. For three months, the famous flyer battled heat, disease, native tribes, and mechanical difficulties along with his two passengers, a photographer and a mechanic. Finally, on February 17, 1926 he set his De Havilland single-engine plane down at Cape Town, his mission successful. He was knighted by King

A Curtiss Pusher was used to publicize an early "aeroplane" mail service experiment in the northwest.

George for his feat. Shortly thereafter, regular mail and passenger service began over the 8,000-mile route.

One of the most interesting airmail experiments authorized by the U.S. Post Office Department was the aerial pickup and delivery mail system carried out by All American Aviation, Inc. The purpose of the experiment was to determine if small towns without airports could receive airmail service by having the incoming mail bags dropped and the outgoing mail bags collected by a snatching device whereby the plane would swoop down, pick up the mail, and fly to the next point.

Two routes were authorized, both using Pittsburgh, Pennsylvania, as the main base. One route was from Pittsburgh to Philadelphia with 27 intermediate pickup points. The other was from Pittsburgh via 28 intermediate points in Ohio and Pennsylvania to Huntington, West Virginia. The combined routes totaled 845 miles over rough terrain that the original airmail pilots had called the "Hell Stretch." The combination of mountains and weather in this area had claimed more lives of pilots over the years than any other stretch in the world.

The "Triple A" organization, headed by Richard DuPont, invoked some of the strictest requirements for their personnel ever heard of up to that time. The inherent dangers of flying among the mountains to get to small towns nestled in the valleys on a regular schedule were evident. If the route were to be successfully flown, it would take good men to do it.

Pilots applying for jobs with All American had to have a minimum of 4,000 flying hours and ten years' experience. The flying mechanics needed an up-to-date Aircraft and Engine Mechanic's license and complete familiarity with the Stinson Reliant monoplanes to be used for the pickup routes. An additional requirement was that all flying personnel had to be natives of the area over which they were to fly. As can be imagined, there were few men in aviation at the time who could qualify for consideration.

When the personnel were chosen, training began. Pickup points were chosen in the 55 towns to be served, which were invariably on high points because of the notorious ground fogs that formed in the low spots. As a result, the points were located in pastures, public parks, school yards, golf courses, and even cemeteries.

The pickup stations consisted of two steel poles, 30 feet high, set 60 feet apart. A rope was stretched between the poles and attached to them by a "transfer clip." The mail bag was connected to the rope in the center.

Pilots were trained to fly directly between the poles. Trailing behind the plane was a cable with a four-fingered grapple. If the pilot were at the correct altitude as he passed over the poles, the grapple would snatch the transfer rope, the mail bag would be released to the grapple, and the mechanic would hand-wind the winch and reel the bag in.

The snatch operations began officially on May 12, 1939. The first five pilots were Sir Holger Hoiriis, Thomas Kincheloe, James Piersol, Norman Rantoul, and C.D. Vinet, with Raymond Elder and Lloyd Julson as reserve pilots. The first piece of mail snatched that day was a package at Latrobe, Pennsylvania, addressed to Postmaster General James T. Farley. The package was dropped at Morgantown, West Virginia, where it made connections on a main airline route to Washington. The plane was Stinson NX2311, which is now in the National Air and Space Museum.

From the pilots' standpoint, the experiment was unique. There were no weather minimums specified by either the Government or the company during the first year's experiment. As long as the pilots stayed within eye contact of the ground and flew only during daylight hours, they could fly at any altitude and in any weather conditions. Each pilot decided for himself when and how he would fly.

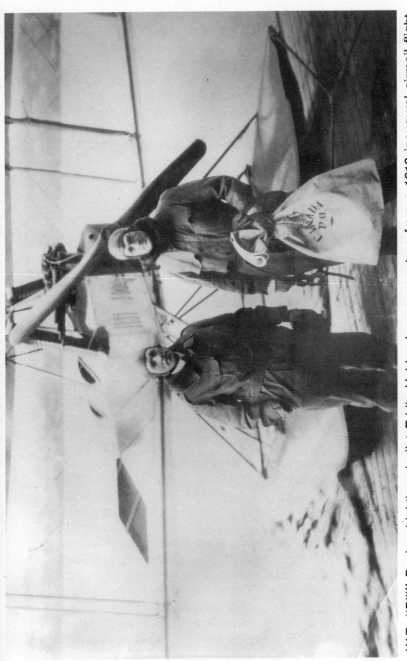

W.E. "Bill" Boeing (right) and pilot Eddie Hubbard pose on return from a 1919 inaugural airmail flight between Seattle and Vancouver. On October 15, 1920, Hubbard made the first international airmail flight between Seattle and Victoria, British Columbia. The route operated almost daily for the next seven years.

As could be expected, there were accidents as the aerial pickup service was being perfected. The pilots were going to try to get the mail through, regardless of weather. During the first year of operations, All American Aviation made over 23,000 pickups and lifted 75,000 pounds of mail plus an additional 6,500 pounds of air express packages. While the exact percentage of flights made compared with those scheduled is not known, it was high and far above that expected by the Post Office Department.

Flying without radio aids to navigation in an area known for its low ceilings and poor visibility, the pilots developed their own techniques for getting the mail through. Since they couldn't see ahead very well most of the time, they learned to fly their routes by looking straight down. Flying at 110 miles an hour, they knew their routes by heart and flew entirely by reference to local landmarks. A row of haystacks, a crossroad, a stand of trees, a barn, or an odd-shaped pasture might not seem magnificent to non-pilots, but to these men they could mean that a pickup point was dead ahead, a turn should be made, or a pull-up was necessary to avoid some obstacle to flight such as a hill, high tension lines, or a tall building. To the few observers ever permitted to go along on these flights, the operation seemed miraculous because pickups and drops would be made without anything apparently being visible on the ground.

After the one year of experimental operation was successfully completed, Richard DuPont, president of the company, recommended to the Post Office Department that the aerial pickup and delivery system his pilots had perfected should be extended to every other section of the country. The recommendation was not adopted; however, All American was granted a certificate "to engage in air transportation with respect to property and mail," in July, 1940—the first airline to be authorized under the new Civil Aeronautics Act, and the only airline authorized to carry mail and express but no paying passengers.

The rapid growth of feeder airlines after the war persuaded the Post Office Department to cancel the All American Aviation contract. However, the lessons learned in the pickup system were not lost. By a refinement of this system, Air Force planes have airsnatched capsules of the Discoverer satellite program as they parachuted to earth after their vital space data-collecting missions. And the human retrieval system has also been perfected so that rescues of stranded personnel can be made by an aircraft in flight using almost the identical system perfected by All American Aviation in 1939.

The "Triple A" pilots never realized that their pioneering of the mail snatch system would someday lead to the retrieval of space capsules and people. They only thought of it in terms of mail bags and mail service to hundreds of small towns throughout the country. But their airmail pioneering influence may not be over yet. The first moon explorers will certainly want to send and receive mail. The retrieval system used both on the earth and on the moon will no doubt be a space-age variation of the original All American Aviation system.

An unusual kind of airmail first was the delivery of psychological warfare messages from enemy aircraft to a civilian populace on the ground. Today, this is called "psychological warfare" and is intended to demoralize an enemy by instilling fear and panic. Lieutenant Max Immelmann of the German Air Force has the honor of being the first deliverer of psychological messages.

Sweeping over Paris in September, 1914, just at sundown, he dropped sandbags containing the following message:

GENS DE PARIS!
LIVREZ VOUS A NOUS!
LES ALLEMANDS SONT A VOS PORTES!
DEMAIN VOUS SEREZ A NOUS!

(People of Paris! Surrender! The Germans are at your gates! Tomorrow you will be ours!)

These "airmail" messages were indeed terrifying to the Parisians. The German army had advanced to within 30 miles of the City of Light. Unfortunately for the Germans, the Parisians did not panic. The French fought all the harder because of them, and the Germans were repulsed. The messages became much sought-after airmail souvenirs.

It was inevitable that someone would eventually want to achieve an airmail "first" in a glider. What is surprising, perhaps, is that such a flight did not take place until 1935. On June 29th of that year, 1,500 letters mailed in Akron, Ohio, were landed by glider at Columbus, after a hazardous one hour and 40-minute flight.

The pilot on this flight was William Bodenlos. He was accompanied by Willis Sperry, later a pilot for American Airlines. The flight had been approved by the Post Office Department as an experiment to determine whether towed gliders might be used for carrying the mail. The thought was that an airplane, loaded with mail, could also tow a glider loaded with mail. Enroute, the glider could be cut loose to land at one airport while the plane could continue to another.

The glider chosen was one designed by Dr. Frank Gross, a Goodyear engineer. It was of sturdy construction, the first four-passenger glider in the world.

Trouble developed soon after take-off. Possibly because the tow plane was underpowered, neither it nor the glider it pulled could gain much altitude. As the pilot leveled off, he gained excessive speed—a speed beyond the limits of the glider. Bodenlos and Sperry became concerned when the airspeed indicator approached the red line, but they couldn't signal the pilot.

The glider began to sway dangerously. At one point, it tipped over on its side and the windshield blew off. Bodenlos related afterward that "we decided to try to unhitch and land but the hitching hook stuck and we couldn't get loose from the tow line until the tow plane slowed down and it was time to land at the Port Columbus airport." The glider was damaged in landing but the mail was delivered. Although it was another airmail "first," it was also a "last." This pioneer flight proved that gliders were not practical air vehicles for flying the mail.

Another air vehicle that was slightly more successful than the glider—but which is now nonexistent—was the autogyro. Built by the Kellett Autogyro Company of Philadelphia, the strange-looking plane was a hybrid that looked like a cross between a wingless airplane and today's helicopter. Since the Postmaster General was authorized "to experiment with new and supplemental means of transporting mail by air," it was decided to give the autogyro a chance to haul mail from the airport at Camden, New Jersey, to the roof of the main post office building in downtown Philadelphia. The first autogyro mail delivery to a post office took place May 25, 1935, when pilot Louis Levy landed on the roof of the Market Street Post Office and handed a sack of mail to Postmaster General James A. Farley.

In 1939, Eastern Airlines was given a contract for a year's experimental operation, and the first regular service began on July 1, 1939. During the year, the autogyro proved reasonably the safe except in high winds. Since it needed a little take-off and landing distance, the crowded building area did not give the pilots much room for error. No profit was being shown on the operation, and after a 'gyro fell off the roof, the experiment was concluded.

Credit for the first delivery of mail by helicopter goes to Colonel H. Franklin Gregory. It was his duty during World War II to be a test pilot of the world's first military helicopter—the Sikorsky YR-4. Anxious to prove to the public what it could do and how much better it was than the unsuccessful autogyro, Sikorsky had wangled permission for Gregory to be the first to deliver mail in his peculiar, ungainly flying machine. On the morning of May 16, 1943, a quarter of a century after the first official airmail flights, Gregory took off from Washington National Airport in a dense fog. His destination was the Capitol, where Speaker of the House Sam Rayburn would be waiting to hand him a packet of mail.

Gregory had received the reluctant permission of the C.A.A. to make the flight. All other air traffic was grounded because of the zero-zero weather conditions, but Gregory convinced the chief C.A.A. inspector that a helicopter could operate "even when the birds won't fly." Gregory described the flight:

Halfway across the field, and the (airport) administration building was enveloped in the fog. It just vanished from sight. This *was* murky weather. Nobody but a fool or a helicopter pilot would fly in anything like this. We were inching our way. Literally feeling our way above the ground. Airport, runways, boundary lights, the edge of the field, finally the Potomac River was directly beneath the ship. I crossed the Potomac to the east bank, then followed its shoreline to the Anacostia River, then up the Anacostia to the Eleventh Street Bridge. It was difficult to see far ahead. Only by straining, it seemed, was it possible to make out the landmarks so clothed in still, mysterious, gray fog, so thick that the rotor blades seemed to slice through it, leaving a pathway in the air.

Now I was flying so low up Eleventh Street that driving a car wouldn't have been much closer to the ground. Pennsylvania Avenue came underneath and I turned left, knowing that ahead in this fog was the Capitol. I was anxious to know just how good visibility was, so I kept a keen eye open for the Capitol dome. Soon, I thought I saw it towering through the mist. I was wrong. That was the dome of the Library of Congress building. But right ahead was the Capital dome, and I eased the YR-4 to a dead-stop landing on the pavement right in front of the building steps.

Since Gregory was fifteen minutes early and there were so many spectators present with cameras, including the news media, he put on a demonstration of what the helicopter could do. He made quick vertical take-offs and flew backwards and sideways to prove its maneuverability.

Promptly at 9:30 A.M. Speaker Rayburn appeared. Gregory put on a short demonstration for him, then hovered about a foot off the ground. Rayburn handed the packet of letters to Gregory. A few minutes later, after picking his way back through the mist the way he had come, Gregory landed at Washington National Airport where he turned the letters over to postal authorities for dispatch by regular air transport. In the words of Gregory himself, "the helicopter, for the first time in history, had carried the mail."

After the helicopter had made its epic airmail flight in 1943, it appeared that this was the end of the fascinating saga of the transport of mail by air. Mail had been flown by pigeons, balloons, dirigibles, airplanes, gliders, autogyros, and helicopters. Was man going to be able to invent any new means of conveying himself through the air? Wasn't there a limit to how high, fast, and far an airplane could be propelled through the air?

By the time that Colonel Gregory made his historic flight, a new means of propulsion had been devised. Airplanes would no longer be limited in speed and altitude to the efficiency of the gasoline engine and steel propellers. Kept as a military secret until the closing days of the war, the jet engine had been designed, perfected, and flown.

The first jet-propelled airplane to transport mail was the P-80 Shooting Star jet fighter plane. On June 22, 1946, Air Force Captain Robert A. Baird III departed Schenectady County Airport, New York, and arrived at Washington National Airport 49 minutes later. He carried a letter to President Harry S. Truman commemorating the event. Another P-80, piloted by Major Kenneth O. Chilstrom, carrying a letter for Orville Wright, arrived at Chicago after a stop at Wright Field, Ohio, in 2 hours and 20 minutes.

By 1948 jet aircraft were becoming a common sight across the country. It was perfectly natural, therefore, that on May 15, 1948, the 30th anniversary of the first official airmail should be commemorated by United States Air Force pilots flying the mail over the same routes their Air Service predecessors had flown three decades before.

At 3:00 P.M. on that date, Captain Vermont Garrison stowed a mail bag away on his P-80B Lockheed Shooting Star that he had been given by Postmaster General Donaldson. A few seconds later, Garrison tucked up the wheels of his fast fighter and headed away from Washington. At the same moment, Lieutenant Colonel Jacob W. Dixon left Idlewild Airport, New York. Twenty-eight minutes later, both planes were on the ground at their destinations. This time, compared with the 3 hours and 20 minutes of flying time that it took the original pilots in 1918, was a reminder of how far aviation had progressed in the intervening years.

While the flights of Baird, Chilstrom, Garrison, and Dixon did not mark the beginning of regular jet airmail service, they did presage the day when jet aircraft would criss-cross the world flying mail and passengers at speeds approaching the speed of sound. The Jet Age was quickly replaced by the Space Age, and a new chapter had already begun in the never-ending story of flight.

=== 9 ===

AIRMAIL PHILATELY

THE WORD "PHILATELY" comes from the Greek words *philos* (loving) and *ateleia* (exemption from tax). In English today the word means the collection and study of postage stamps and stamped envelopes or just stamp collecting in general.

There is evidence that stamp collecting began shortly after the world's first adhesive postage stamps were issued in England in 1840. The first stamp, designed by Henry Corbould, was known as the "Penny Black." It consisted of a drawing of Queen Victoria with the words "Postage" at the top and "One Penny" at the bottom.

The first country to issue stamps on the European continent was Switzerland when, in March, 1843, four- and six-rappen stamps were issued for letters to be sent within the city of Zurich and its suburbs. Brazil was the first country in the Western Hemisphere to print and distribute adhesive stamps. In July, 1843, this Latin-American nation issued three black stamps.

The United States began the issuance of official postage stamps in May, 1845, when the postmaster of New York City, Robert H. Morris, sold the first five-cent stamp. It consisted of a sketch of George Washington encircled by the words "New York Post Office, Five Cents." Although this stamp was printed and issued on Morris' own initiative, it has been accepted as an authentic stamp by the Post Office Department. It was not until 1847, however, that the United States Congress passed an Act which stated that "to facilitate the transportation of letters by mail, the Postmaster General be authorized to prepare postage stamps, which, when attached to any letter or packet, shall be evidence of pre-payment of the postage."

The first two stamps were of five-cent and ten-cent denominations and carried the likenesses of Benjamin Franklin and George Washington respectively. These stamps were in use throughout the country for four years until the rates were reduced in 1851. Printed under contract to civilian firms, it was not until 1894 that the production of United States stamps was taken over by the Bureau of Engraving and Printing under the Department of the Treasury.

As stamps became more plentiful, in the 1850's and 1860's, people in Europe and America began to collect and trade them as a hobby. As the years passed, those bitten by the bug got more serious about their collections. Variations in engraving, color, watermarks, size of perforation holes, and cancellation were studied minutely. Soon specialists in certain issues or classifications of stamps developed, and by the end of the 19th century, postage stamp collecting was a universally accepted pastime which had captured millions of followers throughout the world. It had become a business, too, and as collectors split up into specialty groups, many avid collectors became middle men and bought or sold stamps for others on the world market at a profit. Newspapers started to run articles appealing to this special hobby, pamphlets were printed, and soon catalogs and stamp albums were published which enabled the hobbyist to learn what his stamps were worth and what stamps he needed to make his collection complete.

By World War I, governments all over the world recognized that the interest of stamp collectors was so great that it meant extra income for their respective treasuries. Hobbyists bought stamps but did not use them for the most part. Millions more were bought than ever were used. Thus, many nations issued stamps as a source of income for special purposes. For example, France issued "semi-postal" stamps which were intended partially for charitable purposes such as issues for the relief of victims of World War I, to benefit children of the unemployed, to build monuments, to aid refugees, to buy cigarettes for French seamen, and aid indigent musicians. Nazi Germany issued stamps for propaganda purposes as well as for revenue before and during World War II.

Since postage stamp collecting had become big business, it was only natural that the issuance of airmail stamps would cause many collectors to specialize in them. Just as the pigeon post preceded the airplane, so, too, were pigeon post stamps the first airmail stamps.

New Zealand can claim the honor of this unusual airmail "first," where, in the 1890's, pigeons were used to carry messages between Great Barrier Island and Auckland, a distance of 65 miles. As the result of pigeon races between the two places, S. Holden Howie began the Great Barrier Pigeongram Service in November, 1897, which was fully authorized by the New Zealand Post Office officials. Messages were written on tissue paper and for a shilling would be flown from the copper mines at Great Barrier across the Hauraki Gulf to Auckland. The service became so well accepted and used that postage stamps were issued in 1898. A rival company began operation the next year and issued its own stamps which, due to a misunderstanding between the entrepreneur and the printer, were larger and heavier than the tissue letters themselves. Still another pigeon post which had its own stamps began in 1899 between Marotiri Island and Auckland. This postal service became so popular that by 1901 the New Zealand government laid a cable between Great Barrier Island and Auckland and the pigeon post was discontinued. Today, however, the first airmail stamps ever issued bring an exceptionally high price on the world stamp market.

When airplanes came into practical use and airmail exhibition flights were made, only regular postage stamps were used in the proper amount. Special cachets were designed and printed on "first day covers," and special cancellation overprints were sometimes used.

The first stamp in the world to be placed on mail that was to be carried by air was the "Buffalo Balloon" stamp. Issued by private backers in the United States, it was intended for mail carried by a balloon piloted by "Professor" Samuel Archer King. At least one flight carrying mail was made from Gallatin, Tennessee, to Harrodsburg, Kentucky, on June 18, 1877. There are three known covers with Buffalo Balloon stamps affixed existing today. Each is worth approximately $6,000.

Another unofficial airmail stamp that has become valuable with the passage of time is a black 25-cent stamp printed by the manufacturers of a soft drink. In August, 1911, the *Scientific American Magazine* offered a $50,000 prize to the first person flying a heavier-than-air machine from coast to coast. Cal Rodgers, whose flight was recounted in a previous chapter, piloted his plane "The Vin Fiz Flyer" from Sheepshead Bay, New York, to Long Beach, California, but missed out on the prize money because he couldn't complete the flight within the specified time period.

To finance the flight, the Vin Fiz Company had designed the stamp for Rodgers' souvenir post cards. It shows a biplane in flight and has an inscription which reads "Rodgers Aerial Post Vin Fiz Flyer." Only a few of these unofficial stamps exist today, but each is worth hundreds of dollars.

The first airmail stamps issued for the exclusive use of mail going by air between points was that of the United States for its first official flights of 1918. From that time on, almost every pioneering flight of any consequence carried mail. The famous flight of Alcock and Brown across the Atlantic in 1919 was one of those magnificent "firsts," but the envelopes they carried bore the regular 15-cent Cabot stamp overprinted in St. John's, Newfoundland, with the words "Trans-Atlantic Airpost—$1." Other flights such as those made by the United States Army Air Service around the world in 1924, by Post and Gatty around the world in 1931, and by Byrd and Amelia Earhart all carried envelopes with ordinary postage stamps instead of airmail stamps.

While the flights themselves did not carry mail with airmail stamps affixed, most of the significant pioneering flights of the Golden Age of Aviation have been memorialized afterward on stamps. Over 10,000 different stamps have been issued by the nations of the world honoring not only the pioneers themselves but the planes they flew, aeronautical inventions, and even the museums where the memorabilia of these pioneers now rests.

The flight of Charles A. Lindbergh across the Atlantic in May, 1927, publicized aviation like no other aviation feat had before. Although a mail pilot himself, he carried no mail on his epic trip. However, his feat was recognized by the adoring public of a dozen nations on their stamps afterward. It was then that other nations issued airmail stamps honoring their own air heroes: Germany with stamps honoring the Zeppelin flights; Italy, the Balbo flights; France, the famous cross-channel flight of Bleriot. Some countries remembered brave airmen who failed and died trying to set records or establish aviation "firsts."

Through the years since the 1920's, governments have fully recognized that stamp collecting is big business and advertise the issuance of new stamps with all the techniques known to modern man. In the United States, over 100,000,000 copies of a commemorative stamp may be printed and sold and airmail commemoratives are no exception, although the number of different airmail stamps issued is quite small.

Since the airlines of many foreign nations are run by their respective governments, many take the opportunity to advertise the lines, the airplanes they fly, or planes made in their countries. Russians use engravings featuring the various Tupolev and Ilyushin aircraft in use on Aeroflot. France features its Caravelle transport and Alouette helicopter. Switzerland is proud of its DH-3 Haefeli transport and its Zoegling training glider. However, since many nations fly American-built planes over their routes, these craft are also featured. For example, the KLM Airline of the Netherlands featured the Douglas DC-8; the Belgians have used the Douglas DC-4's and Boeing 707's; the Swiss have engraved the likeness of the Douglas DC-3 and DC-4 and the Lockheed "Orion."

The United States, probably to avoid an accusation of partiality by seeming to advertise one make of plane over another, has steered a different course. The tendency is to have an engraving that is a composite of several aircraft that are not recognizable as those of any particular manufacturer. Notable exceptions, of course, are the first airmail stamp which showed the De Havilland biplane, the "Spirit of St. Louis," the China Clippers of the late 1930's, and the Douglas four-engine DC-4. Two fighting planes, the Boeing B-52 and the Lockheed F-104, are also exceptions.

Now that airmail stamps of the world have become so plentiful, a fair share of the world's estimated 40,000,000 stamp collectors have further compartmentalized their interests. Many now specialize in stamps, or cachets, featuring particular aspects of aviation such as "first" flights, lighter-than-air, jet planes, helicopters, space flights, and rocket mail.

=10=

MISSILE MAIL

THE FIRST PERSON known to have suggested the idea of propelling mail by some explosive means from one place to another was the editor of the *Berliner Abendblatter (Berlin Evening News)*, Heinrich von Kleist. In an issue dated October 10, 1810, von Kleist wrote an article entitled "Preliminary Thoughts About Mortar Mail." The purpose of the article was to propose a system of conveying messages from one place to another that was better than the semaphore system then in use. The semaphore system was dependent on good visibility between stations and thus could not be used in bad weather or at night. Even when working perfectly, it was completely inadequate for the transmission of long messages, official documents, reports, or "useful enclosures" such as money.

Von Kleist editoralized that an all-weather system was needed and that his proposal ought to work "at least within the confines of the civilized world." He envisioned a number of artillery batteries stationed between cities that would fire hollow shells loaded with letters and post cards instead of explosives. The mail loads would be propelled from one battery to another, retrieved, and fired to the next. "As a quick computation will show," von Kleist wrote, "a letter dispatched by this means would cover the distance from Berlin to Stettin (75 miles) or to Breslau (180 miles) in half a day, or in about one-tenth the time required by a mounted courier."

Von Kleist was ahead of his time. It was over a century before the next proposal to convey mail through the air by this means was again seriously proposed. In 1926, Dr. Robert H. Goddard

Chapter 10

built and fired the world's first successful liquid-fuel rocket. This success was as epochal in the history of flight as the first flight of the Wright Brothers, for it presaged the beginning of the Space Age. Scientists the world over began to look beyond the earth's horizons and into space. Then imaginations, unfettered by this new means of propulsion that was now within the realm of possibility through Goddard's experiments, began to foresee new adventures. Two of these scientists were Dr. Franz von Hoefft and Professor Hermann Oberth, charter members of the *Verein fur Raumschiffart* (Society for Space Travel). These men were good friends and exchanged scientific ideas liberally in the 1920's and 1930's. It is possible that credit belongs to both of them for the idea of missile mail, but Dr. von Hoefft is on record as having proposed such a possibility first in a paper he read before the Society in February, 1928. One of the rockets he proposed to build would carry a mailbag in the upper stage, he said, which would "be capable of reaching any point of the globe, along a Keplerian ellipse, in about an hour."

Later that same year, Oberth delivered a lecture to the Scientific Society for Aeronautics in Zoppot in which he also proposed missile mail. He suggested the building of small rockets with automatic guidance systems that could travel 600 to 12,000 miles carrying 22 to 44 pounds of mail. He felt that an error of only a few miles in the landing point could be possible. As translated by Willy Ley in his excellent book, *Missiles, Moonprobes and Megaparsecs*, Oberth said:

> This rocket, therefore, seems suitable for transporting urgent mail over long distances in a very short time. The rocket would have to land by means of a parachute; some other means of transportation would then carry the apparatus to its precise destination. At a later date I would equip such a rocket with a powerful booster stage that would result in transoceanic ranges.

Oberth did not build the mail rockets he proposed. It remained for Austrian engineer Friedrich Schmiedl, who never heard of Oberth or von Hoefft's proposals, to claim the missile mail "first." Living in the Austrian Alps, Schmiedl realized that his countrymen, isolated by the towering mountains, needed a faster means of mail delivery. Working alone, he constructed six rockets which he labeled V-1 through V-6 and invented a parachute release that would lower the payload safely to the ground when the rockets' energy was expended. He fired all six rockets

Missile mail experiments were carried out by the U.S. Navy with the radio-controlled Regulus I in 1957. The first officially recognized missile mail was flown in a Regulus I from a submarine off the coast of Florida on June 8, 1959.

with varying degrees of success. His V-7, the first to carry mail, was successfully launched on February 2, 1931. It carried 102 cards and letters from Schockel over a 4,600-foot mountain to Radegund, where the burned out rocket parachuted gently to earth with the mail unharmed. Other shots followed, including one at night on October 28, 1931, from Grazerfeld to St. Peter. In all, Schmiedl fired 25 mail rockets between 1931 and 1935, most of which were entirely successful.

Another missile mail experimenter was Reinhold Tiling, a German who successfully fired a rocket containing 188 postcards near Hanover on April 15, 1931. Another German interested in sending mail by rocket was Gerhard Zucker, whose experiments were largely failures.

One interesting and successful flight, out of a number of missile mail experiments undertaken, occurred in India on June 29, 1935. On that date a missile nicknamed "David Ezra" was fired across the Damoodar River. In addition to 189 specially

printed postcards, it carried a rooster and a hen named Adam
and Eve. The two birds were uninjured and the mail unharmed.
Thus, one of the first missile mail flights became another missile "first"—the transport of living animals by rocket. The experimenter was Stephen H. Smith, who had the honor of being the
first to fire a mail rocket in India. He achieved many other firsts
in the years between 1935 and 1944. For example, he was the
first to rocket a snake, whiskey, medicines, advertising messages, food, newspapers, cigarettes, propaganda messages,
mice, and photographs. In addition, he fired the first boomerang
rocket which returned to its launching site and glided to earth
unharmed. He made several hundred firings, and most of these
carried mail.

In the United States, the first rocket mail flight was made
February 23, 1936, at Greenwood Lake, New York. The inventors
of this missile, the *Gloria*, were Willy Ley, Louis Goodman, and
Hugh F. Pierce. A curious device, it was 11 feet long with a 15-
foot wingspan. The rocket carried 6,149 letters and post cards
upon which were affixed specially printed rocket stamps in addition to regular postage.

Elsewhere in the United States, Keith E. Rumbel achieved
an airmail "first" which has been lost in the passage of time. In
June, 1936, he made several experimental mail rocket flights
from McAllen, Texas. Then, on July 2nd, Rumbel set up his
apparatus outside the town and loaded 2,000 envelopes aboard
five rockets, all marked with a special inscription:

FIRST INTERNATIONAL
ROCKET FLIGHT
FROM
THE GARDEN OF GOLDEN GRAPEFRUIT
OVER THE SILVERY RIO GRANDE
TO
SCENIC AND HISTORIC MEXICO

The flights, sponsored by McAllen's American Legion Post #
37, were short but significant. Although one of the rockets
exploded in the air, the other four landed safely. (One rocket,
however, hit a house, and the mail was seized by Mexican
authorities.) As soon as the rockets were launched across the
river to the outskirts of Reynosa, Mexico, Rumbel and his entourage of Legionnaires walked across the International Bridge and
promptly readied them for return flights. Without wasting any
time, Rumbel fired the rockets, which made his flights the first

return international missile mail flights. Two thousand letters were launched from Reynosa to McAllen; however, two rockets were damaged in flight and the letters scattered over the countryside.

Just as balloons, artillery, and airplanes had been used to drop propaganda and "Surrender or Die" messages to enemy troops, so it was inevitable that rockets would be used for this same kind of "airmail." The first rockets to be used for this purpose were fired during the Spanish Civil War in 1936. The forces of Generalissimo Francisco Franco fired missiles at enemy advance posts. Written in both Spanish and Arabic, the messages pointed out the criminal intentions of the enemy leaders and demanded the troops give up to Franco's forces. The opposing forces also used propaganda rockets on several occasions.

The Germans used missiles to spread thousands of leaflets over Copenhagen and other Danish cities on April 9 and 10, 1940. The messages announced the occupation of Denmark and warned the Danes against disobeying the laws to be promulgated by the Nazi authorities.

The V-bombs launched against England by the Germans during World War II were also used to spread leaflets. Hoping to demoralize the British military forces and the civilian population, the Germans fired several V-1's carrying scare leaflets in 1944. On Christmas Eve that year, one V-1 dropped a leaflet entitled "V-1 P.O.W. Post" containing facsimiles of letters written by British prisoners languishing in German camps. In January, 1945, a V-1 missile dropped four-page leaflets near Antwerp, Belgium. In one corner of the paper, printed in three languages, was the warning:

GET OUT OF THE WAY OF THE V-1 AND V-2—
THE BOMBARDMENT WON'T STOP!

Other experimenters tried to make history with missile mail flights in the United States, Mexico, Cuba, Australia, France, England, and Holland, but none succeeded with lasting effect. The rockets proved expensive to build, and the expense could not be justified until great distances could be traversed. Just as in the beginning of the official airmail flights between New York and Washington, not enough time was saved to make the expense worth the effort when compared to other means of transportation.

The scientific breakthroughs achieved in missile technology during and after World War II are well known. Air-breathing mis-

siles were developed which were cheaper to construct than liq-
uid-propelled or solid-fuel rockets. They were a sort of
unmanned jet aircraft that, with automatic piloting devices,
could be launched from land or sea and made to land precisely
anywhere, just as piloted airplanes could.

One of the earliest guided missiles was the Regulus I, a sur-
face-to-surface missile which could be fired by United States
Navy ships and submarines against shore targets. The radio-
controlled Regulus I was followed by the Regulus II, an improved
version that could fly at supersonic speeds and high altitudes for
hundreds of miles.

It was the Regulus II that made history on September 16,
1958. The Navy, anxious to prove its capability with new missile, conceived the idea of having it fly from a submarine, the
U.S.S. *Grayback*, off the Pacific coast to Edwards Air Force Base,
California. The occasion was a secret operational firing to test
the new model. Just before take-off, a packet of official United
States Navy mail was placed aboard. No cancellation being
required, there were no formalities of stamping or cacheting
observed.

The Regulus was launched without difficulty and flew its
prescribed course; however, upon arriving over the Muroc Dry
Lake which served as the Edwards Air Force Base runway, the
ground controller could not get the missile to respond to signals
to put down its gear. There was no choice but to bring it in on its
belly. The missile smashed into the ground and immediately
caught fire. To the surprise of everyone, in spite of the fire's
intensity, the mail was recovered intact and sent on its way
through Post Office channels.

Since this flight was secret and the mail bore no stamps and
was not dispatched through official mail channels from its point
of origin, the Post Office Department and philatelists would not
recognize this as the first United States official missile mail. The
Navy decided to try again.

On May 1, 1959, a Regulus I, not then in a classified test status, was launched from the Pacific Missile Range at Point Mugu,
California, and recovered at the same point. One hundred and
fifty envelopes were flown, and among the witnesses were postal
officials from nearby areas. Although United States Navy pen-
alty envelopes were used, seven-cent airmail stamps were
affixed, and the mail sent on its way after a successful landing.
However, for reasons not clear, the Post Office Department also
declined to recognize this flight as an "official" first. The Navy
decided to try once more for this honor.

The Regulus II made airmail history on September 16, 1958, when it was fired from a submarine off the California coast to Edwards Air Force Base. Although this was an airmail "first," it was not recognized by philatelists because it contained official Navy mail that did not go through the Post Office system. A second successful firing on May 1, 1959, was also disallowed. The firing of the Regulus I off the Florida coast on June 8, 1959 is therefore acknowledged as the official "first."

On June 8, 1959, another Regulus I carrying the "United States First Official Missile Mail" was launched from the submarine U.S.S. *Barbero* off the Florida coast. The missile blasted skyward at 9:10 A.M. and landed at the Naval Auxiliary Air Station at Mayport, Florida, 21 minutes later. This time, the mission was "official" in every sense, having been approved personally by President Eisenhower. Postmaster General Arthur E. Summerfield was on hand at the landing site to receive the mail and noted that this experimental flight "is of historic significance to the peoples of the entire world." He added:

Today's shipment of mail by missile has given us extremely valuable information of far-reaching importance to the future of the United States mail service, namely:

1. The use of compartments built into missiles to carry considerable shipments of mail appears highly practical.
2. Significant quantities of mail can be loaded quickly and efficiently into missiles.
3. Missiles can be developed to carry mail safely and swiftly.
4. The relative lightness of letters and the small space they occupy makes them ideal users of missile technology.
5. Guided missiles may ultimately provide a solution to problems of swifter mail delivery for international marts, for isolated areas where other transportation is infrequent, as well as a supplementary high-priority service to big population centers.

Three-thousand letters were delivered via Regulus I bearing the wording "First Official Missile Mail—U.S. Post Office Department." A cancellation reading "U.S.S. *Barbero*" with date and approximate time of launch was placed on the cover.

Summerfield concluded the activities on that day in 1959 by saying:

In colonial days Benjamin Franklin took the mails from horseback and put it on coaches; in 1831, the Post Office Department was the first to use the "new fangled" trains; in 1858, the Post Office linked the nation with the famous Overland Mail stage service to be followed in 1860 with the even faster Pony Express. In 1918, when most people still thought the airplane an unworkable contraption, the Post Office Department demonstrated its practical peacetime uses with the first regular airmails.

Today's Missile Mail will go down in history as another saga of progress and achievement in our national heritage.

Has the saga of the airmail ended with the Regulus flight? With all of our genius for sending electronic signals into space, have we seen the end of the need for sending old-fashioned letters and post cards from one point to another? With satellites, television, and the marvels of photographic reproduction, will the day come soon when we will no longer need to send handwritten symbols from one person to another?

Don't bet on it. For where man goes, so goes the need for privacy in his communications, for the personal touch which his handwriting or his signature conveys. The first man on Mars will probably find a missile mail letter waiting for him when he completes his 34-million mile trip.

The saga of the airmail is not over.

Index

A

Achmed, Caliph of Baghdad, commercial pigeon post under, 2
Acosta, Bert, 130
aeolipiles, balloon steering devices, 30
Aeroflot, USSR, stamps showing planes of, 145
air express shipment, 99, 105, 106
Air Force Museum, Wright-Patterson Air Force Base, 10
airlines and airline-carried airmail, 95-108
  aircraft manufacturers and, 97
  aircraft performance improvements for, 98
  Boeing Air Transport in, 100
  cargo haulage, 105
  China Clippers for, 103
  competition in, 98, 100
  engineering developments of importance during, 98
  foreign airmail contract (FAM), 100, 101
  Panagra airmail route, 101-103
  passengers included with mail, 96
  post-World War II growth of, 105
  pressure pattern flight, 105
  routes developed for, 97
  scheduling reliability for passengers, 98
  stamps for, 145
  trans-Pacific routes for, 103
  transcontinental air-rail service, 96
  transcontinental routes for, 96
  volume of mail delivered by, 1933, 108
  Zeppelin-type dirigibles, first established, 31-32
airmail milestones (see also U.S. airmail)
  autogyro used for, 136

Britain, 34
catapult airmail, 126
distance, speed, endurance records, 126
European exhibition flights of, 34
first exhibition flight, Allahabad, India, 34
France, 34
Germany, 34
glider used for, 135-136
Grahame-White Aviation Company, British, 34
helicopter used for, 136-138
jet aircraft used for, 138-139
London-to-Australia, 128
London-to-South Africa attempt, 130
milestones in, 123-139
navigation techniques, early, 134
pick-up bags tried, 131-135
propaganda delivered via, 135
ship-to-shore delivery, 124-126
transPacific flight, 130
transpolar flights, 128
Airmail Act of 1925, 95
Aisne-Marne offensive (WWI), pigeon post used by U.S., 6
Alaska, first airmail flight for, 1924, 84-88
Alcock, John, first transatlantic airmail flight, 126-128, 144
All American Aviation Inc., 125, 131-135
Allahabad, India, first airmail exhibition flight, 34
Allison, Ernest M., U.S.P.O. Air Mail Service pilot, 90
  first U.S. airmail night flight, 62, 66, 67
Alouette helicopter stamp, 145

Altoona, Pennsylvania, first airmail delivery to, 40
America, ship-to-shore airmail, 124
American Airways, 100, 105
American Export Airlines, 103
American Signal Corps, pigeon post used by, World War I, 6
Ames, Charles H., U.S.P.O. Air Mail Service pilot, 90, 92
Amex, 104
Amundsen, Ronald, 128
Anacreon, "Ode to the Carrier Pigeon," 1
Andridson, Keith V., trans-Pacific airmail, 130
Armour, J. Ogden, first transcontinental flight, 36-39, 143, 144
Army Aerial Mail Service, 48-55
  Belmont Park Race Track as landing field, 46, 47
  first pilots of, 46, 47
  inaugurated 1918, 39, 42, 44, 45, 46
  Lipsner, Benjamin B., administration of, 48-56, 58
Army Air Corps airmail, 107-121
  crashes, 112, 113, 114, 116, 120
  development of, 110-112
  Douglas B-7 bomber for, 109
  funding restrictions on, 115
  ground support inadequacies for, 115-116
  Las Vegas, Nevada operations office, 120
  Martin B-10 bombers used for, 113, 116
  personnel for, 112
  phase-out and end of, 117
  pilot training for, 116-117
  private sector resumes routes of, 120-121
  public outcry against, 114
  radio stations for, 119
  reduction in routes for, 116
  route structure developed for, 112, 115
  speed records set by, 119
  status board, Cheyenne station, 118
  volume of mail delivered by, 119
Army Air Service, 43, 44, 46
Arnold, Henry H., "Hap"
  Army Air Service, 43-44, 46
  early U.S. airmail pilot, 35
  Army Air Corps airmail, 112, 116
Atlantic balloon, first St.Louis-New York flight, 1859, 25-28
Australian pigeon post, 4
autogyro, 129, 136

B

Babylonian pigeon messengers, 1
Baird, Robert A., jet aircraft airmail, 138, 139
Baker, Newton D., Secretary of War, 44, 59
Balbo, 144

Balchen Bernt, 130
banking, use of pigeon couriers in, 2
barnstormers, balloonists, 24
Barry, Gen. William T., xi
Battle of Verdun, pigeon post used during, 5
Beachey, Lincoln, early U.S. airmail pilot, 39
Beck, Paul, early U.S. airmail pilot, 35, 36
Belmont, August, use of Belmont Race Track as landing field, 46, 47
Bently, George, early U.S. airmail pilot, 35
Bismarck, Franco-Prussian war balloon usage, 28
Black, Hugo, 108
Blanchard, Pierre
  first English channel crossing in balloon, 17, 18, 19
  first U.S. balloon flight by, 19-24
  Journal of My Forty-Fifth Ascension, 22
Bleriot, 144
Bodenlos, William, glider airmail flight, 135-136
Boeing 247, 100
Boeing 707 stamp, 145
Boeing Air Transport, 100
Boeing B-52 bomber, commemorative stamps showing, 145
Boeing, W.E. "Bill," 133
Boyle, George L., early U.S. airmail pilot, 39, 45-55
Branch, Harllee, Assistant Postmaster General, 110
Bremen, catapult airmail, 126
Brookins, Walter R., early U.S. airmail pilot, 39, 40
Brown, Arthur W., first transatlantic airmail flight, 126-128, 144
Brown, Walter F., Postmaster General, 96,97, 108, 109
Bruner, Donald L., airplane landing lights developer, 68
"Buffalo Balloon" stamp, 1877, 143
Burleson, Albert S., Postmaster General, 44, 71
Byrd, Richard E., 130, 144

C

Caesar, Julius, carrier pigeon use of, 1-2
Caravelle transport stamp, 145
cargo haulage, 105
carrier pigeons (see pigeon post)
Catalina flying boats, 104
catapult airmail, 126
Chamberlin, Clarence C., ship-to-shore airmail, 126
Chilstrom, Kenneth O., jet aircraft airmail, 138, 139
China Clippers, 103
  commemorative stamps showing, 145
Civil Aeronautics Act of 1938, xi

Civil War, pigeon post used during, 5

Cobham, Alan J., London-to-South Africa airmail, 130

Collins, Marion S., U.S.P.O. Air Mail Service pilot, 77

Colonel Air Transport, 100

Columbus, catapult airmail, 126

Consolidated Aircraft, 104

Consolidated B-24 bomber, airmail aboard, 63

Conte Grande, ship-to-shore airmail, 126

Corbould, Henry, designer of "Penny Black" stamp, 141

Crane Committee, airmail scandal and, 108

crash site, U.S.P.O Air Mail Service biplane, 78, 83

Crisson, Frank, U.S.P.O. Air Mail Service pilot, 80

Culver, Harry, early U.S. airmail pilot, 54

Curtiss Condor, 100

Curtiss "Jennies"
first Washington-New York mail service, 1918, 39, 42, 44-46
Pershing Punitive Expedition, 1916, 40, 43

Curtiss Pusher, 131

Curtiss R-2 airplanes, 43

Curtiss, Glenn, 46, 123

D

Daniel Guggenheim Fund, 96, 108

De Havilland bi-wing trainer, 1918-1927, 59

Deeds, Edwin A., Army Aerial Mail Service, 1918, 46

Deutsche Luftschiffahrts-Aktien-Gesellschaft (DELAG) airline, 31-32

Deutschland I dirigible, 32

DH-3 Haefeli transport stamp, 145

Dickin Medal, wartime animal heroism award, 14

Dietz, H.L., Army Air Corps airmail pilot, 113

dirigibles (see also lighter-than-air airmail)
Deutschland I, 32
early Luftwaffe use of, 31
electric motor for, 31
first airline established using, 31-32
gasoline engine for, 31
Graf Zeppelin, 32
Hindenberg, 32
Zeppelin, Count Ferdinand von, 31
Zeppelin-type, first flight of, 31

Dixon, Jacob W., jet aircraft airmail, 139

dogs, pigeon post birds transported by, 12

Douglas B-18 bomber, pigeon post launched from, 14, 15

Douglas B-7 bomber, 109, 111

Douglas DC-2, 100

Douglas DC-series aircraft stamps, 145

Dragonfly monoplane, first official U.S. airmail plane, 34, 37

DuPont, Richard, airmail pick-up bags, 131-135

Duruof, Jules, balloon air-mail, Franco-Prussian war, 3, 28-30

E

Earhart, Amelia, 144

Eastern Air Transport, 100, 136

Eastham, James Y., Army Air Corps airmail pilot, 112

Eckener, Dr. Hugo, Zeppelin-type dirigibles and, 31-32

Edgerton, James C., early U.S. airmail pilot, 46, 47, 53-57

Egyptian pigeon messengers, 1, 2

Eielson, Carl Ben, first Alaskan airmail flight, 84-88

Eisenhower, Dwight D., 153

Elder, Raymond, 132

Ellsworth, Lincoln, 128

Ellyson, T.G., early U.S. airmail pilot, 35

Ely, Eugene, early U.S. airmail pilot, 35

engines, 98

Europa, catapult airmail, 126

European pigeon post, 2, 5

F

Farley, James A., Postmaster General, 97, 109, 119, 132

First Aero Squadron, Pershing Punitive Expedition, 1916, 40, 43

Fleet, Reuben H.,
Army Aerial Mail Service, 46, 47, 49-55
U.S. airmail pilot, 39, 42-46

float planes, 104

flying boats, 104

Fokkers, 100

Forbes, Robert, early U.S. airmail pilot, 36

Ford Air Transport, 96

Ford Tri-Motor planes, 101

Ford, Henry, private airmail contractor, 96

foreign airmail contract (FAM), 100

Foulois, Benjamin D., 40, 43, 109-120

France, airmail in, 34

Franco-Prussian war
balloons used during, 3, 20, 21, 28-30
pigeon post used during, 3

Franklin, Benjamin, 154

Franklin, William, first air mail letter, 18

French pigeon messengers, 3, 4

French Revolution, pigeon post used during, 3

G

G.I., World War II homing pigeon, 13

Gager, O.A., first St.Louis-New York flight, 1859, 25-28

Gambetta, Leon, Franco-Prussian war balloon use by, 28, 29, 30

Gardner, Ed, early U.S. airmail pilot, 60
Garrison, Vermont, jet aircraft airmail, 138-139
Gatty, 144
Gaynor, William J., 123
Germany
  airmail in, 34
  catapult airmail, 126
  pigeon messengers, 4
gliders, 135-136
Gloria missile mail rocket, 150
Goddard, Robert H., 147
Goldstrom, John, U.S.P.O. Air Mail Service account, 71-75
Goodman, Louis, missile mail experimenter, 150
Goodrich, Arthur W., pigeon post carrier, 9
Graf Zeppelin dirigible, 32
Grahame-White Aviation Company, British airmail, 34
Great Barrier Pigeongram Service, 1897, 4, 143
Great Britain, airmail in, 34
Greek pigeon messengers, 1
Gregory, H. Franklin, helicopter airmail, 136-138
Grenier, J.D., Army Air Corps airmail pilot, 112
guided missiles, 152, 153, 154

H

Haarlem, Siege of (1573), use of pigeon post during, 2
Hall, Howard, pressure pattern flight developer, 105
Hamel, gustave, first airmail flight, 123
Hammond, Edward, early U.S. airmail pilot, 35
Harris, Harold R., lighted airstrip developer, 68
Havens, Beckwith, early U.S. airmail pilot, 39
Hearst, William Randolph, first transcontinental flight, 36-39, 143, 144
helicopters, 136-138
Henderson, Paul, 24-hour U.S. airmail flights, 68-69
Hickman, Horace M., 112
Hindenberg dirigible, 32
Hitchcock, Frank H., Postmaster General, 34, 35, 36, 37, 40
Hoffman, Josef, German airmail initiated, 34
Hoiriis, Holger, 132
homing pigeons (see pigeon post)
Hoover, Herbert C., 97
Howard, Frank L., Army Air Corps airmail pilot, 116
Hoyt, Ross G., Army Air Corps airmail routes, 115

Hubbard Air Transport, 95
Hubbard, Edward, first private airmail contract, 95, 133
Hudgins, D.E., 74
Hyde, first St.Louis-New York flight, 1859, 25-28
Hyde-Pearson, Leonard Brooke, U.S.P.O. Air Mail Service pilot, 92

I

Ile de France, ship-to-shore airmail, 126
Immelmann, Max, 135
Imperial Airways Ltd., 130
India
  airmail in, 34
  pigeon post, 4
International Aviation Meet of 1911, first U.S. airmail exhibit, 34, 35, 36
inverted center 24-cent airmail stamp, 1918, 35, 55, 56

J

Japanese pigeon post, 4
Jeffries, John, first English channel crossing in balloon, 17, 18, 19
Jenny airplane (see Curtiss "Jennies")
jet aircraft, 138-139
John Silver, World War I homing pigeon, 3, 6, 8, 10
Jones, B.Q., 112
Jones, E. Lester, early U.S. airmail mapper, 54
Journal of My Forty-Fifth Ascension, Blanchard, 22
Julson, Lloyd, 132

K

Kaiserin Augusta Victoria, first ship-to-shore airmail, 124
Kellet Autogyro Company, 129, 136
Kelly Act, 69, 95, 107
Kelly, Clyde, 95
Kelly, M.J., 72
Kerwin, Arthur R., Army Air Corps airmail pilot, 116
Kincheloe, Tom, airmail pilot, 125, 132
King, Samuel Archer, balloonist, 143
Kingsford-Smith, Charles, trans-Pacific airmail, 130
Klein, Eugene, stamp collector, 55
Knabenshue, A. Roy, first air express shipment, 1912, 99
Knight, Jack, first U.S. airmail night flight, 62-68
Krebs, Arthur C., first electric motor dirigible flight, 31
Kurstauben (exchange pigeons), banking use of pigeon couriers, 2

L

L-5 liason plane, airmail aboard, 65
Lamountane, John, first St.Louis-New
    York flight, 1859, 25-28
landing lights, 68
Las Vegas, Nevada, Army Air Corps air-
    mail operations office, 120
Leonard, E.C., first U.S. airmail night
    flight, 62
Leviathan, ship-to-shore airmail, 126
Levy, Louis, autogyro airmail, 136
Lewis, W.F., first U.S. airmail night flight,
    62
Ley, Willy, 148, 150
lighted airstrips, 68
lighter-than-air aircraft, 17-32
    American Express Company, first mail
        sent by, 25-28
    barnstormers, 24
    DELAG airline established, 1910,
        31-32
    Deutschland I, 32
    dirigibles, electric motors, 31
    dirigibles, gasoline engines, 31
    early attempts at flight, 24
    early propulsion attempts, 30
    early steering devices for, 30
    first English channel crossing in, Blan-
        chard and Jeffries, 17, 18, 19
    first European mail delivered by, 19
    first transatlantic crossing by, 127
    first U.S. flight of, 19-24
    first U.S. letters delivered by, 19
    Franco-Prussian war use of, 20, 21, 28,
        29, 30
    French air mail service, 29, 30
    Graf Zeppelin dirigible, 32
    Hindenberg dirigible, 32
    homing pigeons launched from, 20
    King, Samuel Archer, early airmail flight,
        143
    pigeon post launched from, 16
    pigeon post vs., 3
    St. Louis-New York flight attempt, 1859,
        25-28
    trans-Atlantic flight attempt, 25
    Zeppelin, Count Ferdinand von, 31
Lindbergh, Charles A., xi, 144
    transatlantic flight by, 108
    U.S.P.O. Air Mail Service duty, 81-84
Lipsner, Benjamin B., 69
    Army Aerial Mail Service administrator,
        48-58
    U.S.P.O. Air Mail Service, 58, 59, 60
Lockheed Electra, 100
Lockheed F-104 fighter, commemorative
    stamps showing, 145
Lockheed "Orion" stamp, 145
Lockheed Vega, Panagra airmail route
    plane, 104
Lowden, Ed, flight mechanic, 125

Lowry, Durnwald O., Army Air Corps air-
    mail pilot, 113

M

MacArthur, Douglas, 111, 116
MacClure, Maj. Thomas, Chief of U.S.
    Pigeon Unit (WWII), 11
Maddux, 100
magnetic compass, early U.S. airmail, 54
maps
    early U.S. airmail, 54
    U.S.P.O. Air Mail Service, 90
Martin B-10 bomber, Army Air Corps air-
    mail plane, 113, 116
Martin, Glenn L., 104
McCarran-Lee Bill (Civil Aeronautics Act of
    1938), xi
McCurdy, J.A.C., first ship-to-shore air-
    mail, 124
McDermott, George F., 114
Meuse-Argonne offensive (WWI), pigeon
    post used by U.S., 6, 8, 10
Miles, Brig. Gen. Nelson A., Civil War
    pigeon post, 5
Miller, John M., 129
Miller, Max, early U.S. airmail pilot, 60
Milling, Thomas, early U.S. airmail pilot,
    35
missile mail, 147-155
    first official submarine launch of, 153,
        154
    first U.S. flight, 150
    Goodman, Louis, 150
    guided missiles, 152, 153, 154
    Indian experiments with, 149-150
    Ley, Willy, 150
    Oberth, Hermann, 148
    Pierce, Hugh F., 150
    propaganda deliveries, 151
    Rumbel, Keith E., 150, 151
    Schmiedl, Friedrich, 148, 149
    Smith, Stephen H., 149-150
    submarine launched missiles, 152, 153,
        154
    Tiling, Reinhold, 149
    V-1 rockets used for, 151
    von Hoefft, Franz, 148
    von Kleist, Heirich, early proponent of,
        147
    Zucker, Gerhard, 149
Missiles, Moonprobes and Megaparsecs,
    148
Mocker, World War I homing pigeon, 10
Morehouse, Max, first air express ship-
    ment, 1912, 99
Morris, Robert H., first postmaster to sell
    stamps, 141
Mouton, B.E., U.S.P.O. Air Mail Service
    pilot, 73, 74, 111
Murray, J.P., first U.S. airmail night flight,
    62

N

Nadar, M. (Felix Tournochan), first French balloon-mail, 29, 30
Napoleon III, Franco-Prussian war balloon usage, 28
Napoleonic Wars, use of pigeon post during, 2
National Air Transport, 100
Neptune hot air balloon, 3
New, Harry J., Postmaster General, 95
night flight
   pigeon post, 11
   U.S. airmail, 62-67
Norge dirigible, transpolar flight attempt, 128
Northwest Airways, 100
Noville, George, 130
Nurredin, Sultan of Baghdad, first commercial pigeon post, 2
Nutter, Farr, first U.S. airmail night flight, 62, 67
NYRBA Airways, 104

O

Oberth, Hermann, rocket scientist, 148
Olympic Games, ancient Greece, pigeons to relay results of, 1
Ovington, Earle L., first official U.S. airmail pilot, 34-37, 123

P

Pan American Airways, 101, 103
Pan American Grace Airways, 101
Panagra airmail route, 101-103
paratrooper, pigeons carried by, 9
Parmalee, Phil O., first air express shipment, 1912, 99, 105, 106
passenger flights (see airlines)
Patrick, Fred J., Army Air Corps airmail pilot, 113
"Penny Black" first issued stamp, 141
Pershing Punitive Expedition, 1916, U.S. airmail planes used in, 40, 43
philately (see stamp collecting)
Pierce, Hugh F., missile mail experimenter, 150
Piersol, James, 132
pigeon post, 1-16
   American Signal Corps (World War I), 6
   ancient use of, 1-2
   Army Air Force of U.S., WWII, pigeon units organized, 11
   Australia, 4
   Babylonia, 1
   balloon launch of, 16
   balloons vs., 3, 20, 21
   banking house use of, 2
   capsule attached to bird's back for, 7
   capsule attached to bird's leg, 8
   Civil War use of, 5
   Dickin Medal recipients, 14
   dogs used to carry birds, 12
   Douglas B-18 bomber launch of, 14, 15
   Egypt, 1, 2
   European use of, 2, 5
   first commercial use of, A.D. 1146, 2
   Franco-Prussian war use of, 3, 20, 21
   French Revolution use of, 3
   German lighthouse use of, 4
   Great Barrier Pigeongram Service established, 1897, 4, 143
   Greece, 1
   hawk attacks on, 4, 5
   India, 4
   Kurstauben (exchange pigeons), banking couriers, 2
   launching procedure for, 11
   military use of, 3
   Napoleonic Wars, 2
   night flight of, 11
   paratrooper carrying pigeon for, 9
   pigeoneers organized, 11
   Poland, 4
   radio telephone vs., 4
   Reuters News Service use of, 3
   Rome, 1
   Russo-Japanese War use of, 4
   scout plane to launch, World War I, 13
   siege of Haarlem (1573), use of, 2
   South African War use of, 4
   stamps issued for, 143
   Syria, 2
   telegraph vs., 3, 4, 5
   training during World War I, U.S., 6
   transatlantic cable vs., 4
   two-way birds, 11
   United States, 4
   whistles to deter hawk attack used, 4
   World War I use of, 5
   World War II use of, 7, 11
pigeoneers, 11, 12
pigeongrams (see pigeon post)
Polish pigeon post, 4
Post, Wiley, 144
Praeger, Otto, 58, 59, 67, 69
President Wilson, World War I homing pigeon, 10
pressure pattern flight, 105
propaganda, 135
Prussian pigeon messengers, 4

R

radio telephone, pigeon post vs., 4
Rantoul, Norman, 132
Reeve Aleutian Airways, 101
Reeve, Robert C., pan-American airmail route, 101-104
Regulus I and II guided missiles, 152, 153, 154
Reliant aircraft, 125, 127
Renard, Charles, first electric motor dirigible flight, 31

Reuter, Paul, telegraphic news service founder, 3
Robey, W.T., stamp collector, 35, 55, 56
Robinson, Hugh
  early U.S. airmail pilot, 39
  ship-to-shore airmail, 124-126, 124
Rodgers, Calbraith P., first trans-continental airmail, 36-39, 143-144
Roman pigeon messengers, 1
Roosevelt, Franklin D., 98, 109, 116
Rothschild, Nathan, use of pigeon post during Napoleonic Wars, 2
Rowe, Harry H., U.S.P.O. Air Mail Service pilot, 72
Rumble, Keith E., missile mail experimenter, 150, 151
Russo-Japanese War, pigeon post used during, 4

S

Schmiedl, Friedrich, missile mail experimenter, 148, 149
Schofield Barracks, Hawaii, 10
Scott, Paul P., U.S.P.O. Air Mail Service pilot, 75-76
Sell, Ernest C., Army Air Corps airmail pilot, 116
ship-to-shore airmail, 124-126
Sikorsky, Igor, 104
Sir, World War II dog transporting pigeon, 12
Smith, Dean C., U.S.P.O. Air Mail Service pilot, 88
Smith, Henry Ladd, 98
Smith, Keith M., 128
Smith, Ross, 128
Smith, Stephen H., missile mail experimenter, 149-150
Smith, Walter J., U.S.P.O. Air Mail Service pilot, 72
Smith, Wesley L.
  first U.S. airmail night flight, 62
  U.S.P.O. Air Mail Service pilot, 71
South African War, pigeon post used during, 4
Spaatz, Carl, Army Air Corps airmail routes, 115
Sperry, Willis, glider airmail flight, 135-136
Spirit of St. Louis, commemorative stamp showing, 145
St. Louis-New York first balloon flight, 1859, 25-28
St. Mihiel offensive (WWI), pigeon post used by U.S., 6
stamp collecting, 141-145
  airline commemoratives, 145
  Austrian 1918 airmail stamps, 56
  Benjamin Franklin, 1847, 142
  "Buffalo Balloon" stamp, 1877, 143
  Bureau of Engraving and Printing production of stamps, 142

experimental U.S. airmail commemoratives, 56
fighters and bombers commemorative stamps, 145
first Army Aerial Mail Service flight, 1918, 53
first British issue, Penny Black, 141
first European issue, Switzerland, 141
first Latin American issue, Brazil, 141
first trans-continental U.S. airmail delivery, 38
first U.S. airmail stamp, Spirit of St. Louis, 145
first U.S. issue, 141
"firsts" commemoratives, 145
flaws and specialty items, 142
foreign flight commemoratives, 144
George Washington, 1847, 142
Great Barrier Pigeongram Service, 143
historic flight commemoratives, 144
hobby begins, 142
inverted center 24-cent airmail stamp of 1918, 35, 55, 56
Italian 1917 airmail stamps, 56
Lindbergh flight commemorative, 144
pigeon post, 143
Postmaster General authorized to issue stamps, 141
"Trans-Atlantic Airpost" stamp, 1919, 144
U.S. airmail, 1900-1918, 33
Vin Fiz Flyer flight commemorative, 143, 144
World War I issues, 142
Zeppelin flight commemoratives, 144
Standard Aero-mail plane, 60
Standard Aircraft Company, 60
Stevenson, Robert Louis, 10
Stinson, Katherine, first female airmail pilot, 123-124
Stout all-metal airplane, 100
Stout, William B., 96
submarine launched missiles, 152, 153, 154
Summerfiedl, Arthur E., missile mail and, 153, 154
Syrian pigeon messengers, 2

T

Taussig, Noah, stamp collector, 53
telegraph, pigeon post vs., 3, 4, 5
Tiling, Reinhold, missile mail experimenter, 149
"tin goose" Stout all-metal airplane, 100
Todd, William A., trans-Pacific airmail, 130
Tournochan, Felix, first French balloon-mail service, 29, 30
Trans World Airlines (TWA), 97
"Trans-Atlantic Airpost" stamp, 1919, 144
transatlantic cable, 4
transatlantic flight
  Lindbergh, Charles A., 108

airmail flight, 144
Transcontinental & Western Air (TWA), 96
Transcontinental Air Transport (TAT), 96, 100
transpolar flights, 128
"Triple A" pilots (see All American Aviation Inc.)
Truman, Harry S., 138

U

U.S. airmail (see also airmail milestones), 57
  Army Air Corps assumes duty of, 107-121
  Crane Committee airmail scandal report, 108
  first official route opened, x
  McCarran-Lee Bill (Civil Aeronautics Act of 1938), xi
  milestones, 123-139
  passengers flying with, xi
  Post Office takes over operations of, x
  private operators take over from Post Office, x
  ship-to-shore delivery, 124
  Stinson, Katherine, first female pilot for, 123-124
U.S. airmail, 1900-1918, 33-56
  Aerial Mail Service, Washington-New York, 1918, 39, 42, 43, 44, 45, 46
  Dragonfly monoplane, first official plane of, 34, 37
  early exhibition and experimental flights, 1912, 39
  early pilots of, 35, 36, 39, 40, 46, 47
  First Aero Squadron, 40, 43
  first exhibition flight, 34
  first official flight of, 52-54
  first payment authorized for, 1916, 40
  first stormy weather flight of, 57-58
  Hitchcock, Frank H., Postmaster General advocating, 34, 35, 36, 37, 40
  maps for, 54
  Ovington, Earle L., first official pilot of, 34, 35, 36, 37
  Pershing Punitive Expedition, 1916, 40, 43
  Post Office Department takes over delivery of, 56
  Rodgers, Calbraith P., first trans-continental delivery, 36-39, 143-144
  World War I development of, 40
  Wright, Orville and Wilbur, 33
U.S. airmail, 1918-1927 (see U.S. Post Office Air Mail Service)
U.S. airmail, private sector (see also airlines), 95-106
U.S. Post Office Air Mail Service, 57-93
  24-hour flight service for, 68-69
  airmail route map, 91
  airplane landing lights developed, 68
  airplane specifications for, 60

Alaskan service inaugurated, 84-88
casualties of, 70
costs of, 70
crash site, 78, 83, 92-93
de Havilland bi-wing plane for, 59, 61
emergency fields established for, 76
first airfields designed for, 60
forced landings, 80, 88-89
Goldstrom, John, written account of flight, 71-75
Kelly Act to turn control to civilian sector, 69
Lindbergh, Charles A., parachute jump by, 81-84
lighted airstrips for, 68
Lipsner, Benjamin B. to organize, 58, 59, 60
maps and route information for, 90
night flights inaugurated, 61-67
parachutes used by, 81-84
phase-out period of, 70
Praeger, Otto to organize, 58, 59
railway link in, 61
record speed achieved, 69
regular night flights begun, 68
Scott, Paul P., westbound night flight report by, 75
training for pilots, 90
transcontinental routes laid out for, 60, 61
volume of mail delivered by, 70
weather information mishaps, 77-80
winter flying gear for, 89
Yager, Frank, stormy weather flight report by, 76-77
U.S.S. Barbero, first official missile mail launch, 153, 154
U.S.S. Grayback, first submarine missile launch, 152
Ulm, P.T., trans-Pacific airmail, 130
Unger, Kenneth, U.S.P.O. Air Mail Service pilot, 88-89
United Air Lines, 100

V

V-1 rocket bombs, missile mail with, 151
Vedrines, Jules, French airmail initiated, 34
Vidal, Eugene, Dept. of Commerce, 110
Vin Fiz, first trans-continental U.S. airmail, 36-39, 143, 144
Vinet, C.D., 132
von Hoefft, Franz, rocket scientist, 148
von Kleist, Heinrich, missile mail proponent, 147
Votaw, Bill, first U.S. airmail night flight, 63, 64, 72

W

Walsh, Charles F., early U.S. airmail pilot, 39

Warner, Edward P., 98
Washington, George, 19, 23, 141
Waters, E.F., Army Aerial Mail Service mechanic, 49, 50, 51, 52
Webster, Jack, first U.S. airmail night flight, 66, 67
Weick, Fred E., engine cowling developer, 98
Western Air Express, 96
Whitbeck, J.E., first U.S. airmail night flight, 67
Whitbeck, John, 72
White, Edwin D., Army Air Corps airmail pilot, 112
Wienecke, Otto, Army Air Corps airmail pilot, 116
William of Orange (1573), use of pigeon post during siege of Haarlem, 2
Williams, W.D., U.S.P.O. Air Mail Service pilot, 72
Wilson, Woodrow, 42, 44, 51
Windham, Capt., first airmail exhibition flight, India, 34
wing loading, 98
Wise, John
  balloon barnstormer, 24
  St. Louis-New York balloon flight, 25-28
Wood, Thurman A., Army Air Corps airmail pilot, 117
World War I
  Battle of Verdun, pigeon post performance, 5
  formal pigeon post training, 6

John Silver, homing pigeon, 3, 6, 8, 10
Mocker, homing pigeon, 10
  pigeon post used during, 5
President Wilson, homing pigeon, 10
  scout planes to launch pigeon post, 13
  U.S. airmail, 1900-1918 development during, 40
  U.S. pigeon post used during, 6
  U.S. pilots trained for, 43, 44, 46
World War II
  British Roll of Honour for pigeon post, 13
  G.I. Joe homing pigeon, 13
  L-5 liason plane, New Guinea airmail, 65
  pigeon post used during, 7, 11
  U.S. Army pigeon units organized, 11
Wright, Orville and Wilbur, 33
Wright-Patterson Air Force Base, Air Force Museum, 10

Y

Yager, Frank
  first U.S. airmail night flight, 62
  U.S.P.O. Air Mail Service pilot, 76-77

Z

Zeppelin, Count Ferdinand von, 31
Zoegling training glider stamp, 145
Zucker, Gerhard, missile mail experimenter, 149

About the Author

Colonel Glines was commissioned and rated as a pilot in the United States Air Force in January, 1942. He subsequently served in a variety of assignments as a squadron and group commander, engineering officer, Air Force ROTC instructor, head of the Department of Defense Magazine and Book Branch and chief of Public Affairs for the Alaskan Command until his retirement in 1968. He flew many types of fighter, bomber and trainer aircraft, including jets, and retains his commercial pilot certificate.

During his Air Force career, Colonel Glines began writing magazine articles and books on a free-lance basis. Upon retirement, he became successively editor of *Air Cargo, Air Line Pilot*, and *Professional Pilot* magazines. His articles have also appeared in many national magazines including *Nation's Business, American Heritage, American Legion*, and *Air Force Magazine*. He has written a number of award-winning books including *The Doolittle Raid, 'Round-the-World Flights, The Legendary DC-3*, and *Jimmy Doolittle: Master of the Calculated Risk*.

Awards include the Lauren D. Lyman Award from the Aviation/Space Writers Association for "excellence in reporting and writing, deep understanding of others, and devotion to the best interests of the aerospace industry." He also received the Max Steinbock Award from the International Labor Press Association for his "humanistic spirit in journalism," in addition to awards from the International Association of Business Communicators, Society of National Association Publications, and the Freedoms Foundation.

9336